PARTNERS IN PREACHING

Clergy and Laity in Dialogue

By the Author:

The Creative Years
Herein Is Love
Man's Need and God's Action
The Miracle of Dialogue
Youth Considers Personal Moods

PARTNERS
IN PREACHING

Clergy and Laity in Dialogue

REUEL L. HOWE

The Seabury Press

New York

Second Printing

Copyright © 1967 by The Seabury Press, Incorporated
Library of Congress Catalog Card Number: 67-20937
Design by Victoria Dudley
581-470-C-15-12.5
Printed in the United States of America

PREFACE

Prevalent among us is a skepticism about the value of the conventional forms of ministry—especially preaching. I concur in this skepticism.

The weakness of preaching stems from its wordiness and monological character. The centuries have been filled with words about Christ. When one stops to think about the volume of words one develops; a sense of horror—words, words, words; words about words, words undoing words; words for the sake of words; words slashing like a blinding blizzard into the face of the world. And at last the world is beginning to cry, "Stop! We can't stand more words. Your words are empty because they are not reinforced by actions that give them authenticity."

But preaching does have power when it is dialogical, when preacher and people become partners in the discernment and proclamation by word and action of the Word of God in response to the issues of our day. Once again the word must become flesh; men must be able to see it as well as hear it.

Giving the word flesh is both the purpose of this book and the task of the church in today's world. The word of the professional preacher by itself is no longer, if it ever

5

was, enough. Men will not hear the conventional sermon. They must see the word acted out; and they themselves must act out the word for others to see. But such action must follow a determined struggle by laity and clergy together to search out the meaning of God's Word for our time.

The church's preaching is a concern for both clergy and laity. Some parts of this book will focus on the layman's role and others on the clergy's part. But each should read the other's parts. Laymen who have responsibility in the church's preaching need to know and understand the ordained preacher's task; and the ordained preacher needs to know and understand the layman's responsibility for the church's preaching. In this way the function of each will complement that of the other. The theme of this book is the whole church's responsibility for making known the Word of God. Out of this joint effort a new kind of preaching will appear.

The insights of this book were born out of discussions with clergy and laity at the Institute for Advanced Pastoral Studies about the problems and possibilities of the church's preaching. In an earlier form these chapters were the Princeton Seminary Alumni Lectures, delivered in September, 1965. I am indebted to all the people who have participated in these discussions for the help and encouragement that they gave me in the formulation of the thesis that I now present.

CONTENTS

PARTNERS IN PREACHING

Clergy and Laity in Dialogue

1

THE CRISIS IN PREACHING

The explosion of technology has produced so many changes in our society that none of us is able fully to keep up with them. As a result of technological advance, we have a whole new set of tools that we never had before. We have also not only new materials, new methods, and new machines, but new levels of education, new standards of living, and new ways of thinking as well.

These changes have reached into every department of our individual lives and into every manner of social organization, the church not excepted. Moreover, these changes have not only set up tensions between the traditional and the new ways of thinking and doing, but they also seem to have robbed certain of our acts of their meaning or else have left us puzzled about how to relate the new to the old. This is not surprising. In every age of change, people act out in their living the tensions and meanings of their age, and they always run the risk of losing traditional insights because they are unable to relate them to the contemporary patterns of their lives.

In order to see specifically just what this can mean in terms of traditional Christian belief and practice, and in terms of the church and the church's preaching, we have only to eavesdrop on three couples at a dinner party who are old friends. Two of these couples are church members; the third has separated from the church. Here is their conversation:

Jack Spread: As an engineer I find it hard to keep up with the technical changes in my own field. My father lived in a world that didn't change very fast. But ours? Phew!

Bill Needham: You're right! And what's more, I'd like to know where we're headed. Everything is changing, but where are we going?

Mary Needham: One thing's not changing, and that's the church, and I'm glad. It's good to have something that's always the same that you can cling to.

Janet Spread: I disagree, Mary. I'm tired of the same old line that we get every Sunday morning. I'd like some help in figuring out what life's all about. Jim Darling, our minister, tries hard. When I talk with him I feel that he understands what our questions and problems are, but when he gets in that pulpit of his, he loses me. Sometimes I think I'll scream from trying to listen to all those meaningless words.

Fred Stickman: Beth and I stood it as long as we could, and then we quit—the church, that is. I couldn't make sense out of the Bible. I don't see why we should accept an antique book as a guide to our life today. And I feel the same about theology. There's something appealing about Jesus, but all that jazz about his being both human and divine gets in my way. All that stuff used to have meaning for people, I guess, but it doesn't have any for me. When I get right down to it, I don't think I need God any more.

Beth Stickman: Nor do I. The church and ministers don't seem to realize that we've grown up and don't need the old religious mumbo-jumbo. What's more, there are a lot of hot issues that are important to me that the church seems afraid to tackle. I refuse to live in two worlds.

Bill Needham: Well, I sure feel as if I live in two worlds. One is the world that began in my childhood: a world of ideas and values learned at home and in Sunday school; and the other is the world I live in now. It's a mixed up world that measures things largely in terms of what works and produces. And I can't get these two worlds together. The church door that Mary and I go through almost every Sunday morning separates rather than connects my two worlds.

Mary Needham: Well, I don't want mine connected. I know Bill and I never agree on these things. When I'm in church I want to feel safe. I want to check my responsibilities and problems at the door. I don't want to think about anything in the outside world that would upset my sense of peace.

Fred Stickman: Damn it, Mary, that's just the point of view that drove me out of the church. I quit because the church didn't speak to my questions and hurts, and I couldn't figure out what the hell they were talking about.

Bill Needham: I agree, Fred, but you're being too hard on Mary. There ought to be a place in religion for refuge, and right now I guess she needs it.

Jack Spread: Sure, sure, we all need security, but what are you going to use your security for if not for facing the insecurities of life? I think the security of religion is for facing the challenges of life and will have to be built in response to the challenges and fears of our own day.

Janet Spread: Good, Jack! Tell them what you were telling me the other night. It made the world we live in sound so exciting.

Jack Spread: I don't know if I can, Janet, but I'll try. We're all in our forties. None of us live in the world we were born in. Even within the last five years discoveries have been made in the fields of medicine, space, science, electronics, sociology, cybernetics, that have stirred some men to think on a new plane which fires their imagination for even more discoveries. The technical progress man is making is like a stampede. It can't be stopped. It'll only get worse. And it makes many past conclusions and methods obsolete. We need help in working out new ones. That's where I would like help from the church.

Bill Needham: That's right! Everything is changing. But as I asked a little while ago: Where are we going? What's the meaning of it all?

Fred Stickman: They're good questions—and ones that we'll have to sweat out as we go along. Certainly the church can't help when it is preoccupied with itself and its obsolete system of ideas and practices. When I used to go to church there were times when the preacher said something that came close to speaking to me. I would like to have followed up on it but there was never an occasion to do so. And then he'd drift into his jargon again.

Bill Needham: You know, that illustrates what I meant earlier when I said that the church door never united the two worlds I live in: the world of values and the world of action.

Jack Spread: Yes! And that's what I'd like—some help in figuring out the meaning of what's happening to us and some fixes for guiding our navigation through these strange waters.

Janet Spread: Honey, I'm afraid you're expecting too much. The clergy we've known are not up to the job and I'm not sure the church is interested. It would have to give up a lot to get its leadership back.

Bill Needham: Wait a minute, now, before we wipe the church off the contemporary map. It exists, millions of people attend services, something must happen. I wonder what difference it does make. Let's ask ourselves: What would we like from the church? Maybe we're looking for the wrong thing.

Mary Needham: Well, I've told you what I want. I'm satisfied!

Janet Spread: Well, I'm not. I'd like our minister to seem not quite so sure he has all the answers. I'd like to feel that he and his church were in this human struggle, too.

Jack Spread: Yes, and I'd like him to use a language I understand, and use illustrations out of my own experience.

Fred Stickman: I'd like some help in exploring the meaning of things and less rehearsing of old creeds. Like Janet, I'd like to have a minister that I felt was using what he believed to deal with present life instead of dragging us back to "religious" times.

This tension, this puzzlement about how to grapple with meaning, has affected not only laymen but also the clergy. If we were to listen in on the luncheon conversation of three young ministers as they discuss on a Monday their experiences of the preceding Sunday, we would hear something like this:

Jim Darling: I asked you to lunch today because I need to talk to somebody. I've about had it. The ministry is damned lonely. I poured out my guts yesterday. It was Whitsunday, you know! I tried to tell my people about the Holy Spirit and they looked as if they couldn't care less. Several of them thanked me for my sermon and said that they "enjoyed" it, but I don't know whether to believe them. They seem concerned about something else. A part of the trouble is that I don't seem to know how to say what I believe in a way that makes sense to them. How do you guys feel about it?

Matt Gilford: I know what you mean. Currently our church suffers from an excessive tendency to look inward rather than outward. The problem is that most of our members, with a few exceptions, don't seem to be really Christian; they see the church as a club, and a dispenser of sermons designed to make them feel good. Some of them are willing to listen to the old whether or not it has any meaning for them. They don't want to think. And they are so damned judgmental. I preach grace to them, but they live by the meanest kind of a law. Preaching is a frustration for another reason, too. I have so many concerns to share with my people but no burning message. Sometimes I feel that my well has run dry.

Jim Darling: I've got some of those ingrown self-righteous church members. But I've some real comers, too —men who are asking real questions. They're involved in some of the most radical experiments and changes of our time. They're looking for answers to some deep questions that our technological age is raising. I talk with them and am fascinated with what they tell me about their thoughts and questions, but when I try to preach the gospel I seem to operate in another world. I can tell that I'm not clicking with them. I'm sure they appreciate my efforts but I detect in them an embarrassed pity for my efforts. Getting across the relevance of God for this age is tough. More and more people seem to get along without him. The stuff I preach sounded good to me in seminary, but my people sure don't listen to me the way I listened to my professors. I wish I knew what's wrong.

Jerry McDuff: I think we have the same problem. And we ministers have the same problem that many of our members have. We've all learned to live in two worlds without any clear connection between them. I feel the pressure of my denomination to have a growing church and the pressure of tradition to preach the true faith; but if I preach the truth and minister to my people, my church might not grow. Already some people have withdrawn their support because of my stand on the question of open housing. I wonder whether the church as an institution will survive in our day as an effective instrument of God.

Jim Darling: Maybe we are being too pessimistic. Our talk depresses me. I need to be picked up, not knocked down! I'd like to learn how to motivate church people; how to stop them from substituting meaningless religious observance for vital worship; how to get them to act as Christians in the world. I'm also fed up with our liturgy. It's dated, and doesn't communicate enough with the modern world.

Matt Gilford: That's right! How do you lead people who want the church to be the way it was "in the good old days" to see things as they really are in our society. One thing I've learned. You can't tell them in so many words. There must be another way. If true, this means that the sermon is passé. Maybe we'll have to find another method than preaching. Many of our best authorities seem to think so.

Jerry McDuff: Well, that doesn't make sense. Think of all the thousands, even millions of people who attend church and who expect a sermon. You can't say to them, "Go home! Your expectations are obsolete." There has to be another answer to the separation between church and society.

Jim Darling: Yeah, maybe there is. But if we don't find

it I predict that in fifty years the irrelevance of the church
will have grown to the point where most people will have
turned away from the church except for the ritual acts
associated with the "hatching, matching, and dispatching"
events of an individual's life. Fifty years ago the churches
in Britain and on the Continent were filled on Sunday,
and now with a few exceptions they're not. The same thing
will happen to us if we don't get on the ball. But how?

These two conversations—the one between laymen and
the other between ministers—clearly focus for us the problem of relationship between the church and the world as
it touches upon the church's preaching responsibility.
There are many in the church, like Mary Needham, who
simply want to cling to old rituals, old formulations of
truth and belief, and old forms of worship and witness
that have hardened into the rigid framework of custom.
And while we may admire their loyalty to the traditional,
we must also be alert to the destructive element that lurks
within it. For, as Raymond L. Bruckberger has observed,
in his book *The History of Jesus Christ,* "It is custom that
destroys us. The evangelical revelation should give us
souls of fire, but custom creates in us the souls of autom-
atons. The words of religion are worn down like peb-
bles, they no longer clash, they no longer wound, they
simply roll with the stream."

In the conversations reported, the laymen are wrestling
with the meaning of their lives and are unable to hear and
understand the preaching of the church; and the preachers
are struggling with the meaning of the gospel with such
exclusive concentration that they are estranged from the
meanings of their people. The results are obvious: There
is no meeting of meaning between the preaching of the
clergy and the experience of the people; and, therefore,

no meeting between the Word of God and the word of man unless it occurs independently of the efforts of the preachers, which, of course, should also be expected.

This bypassing of meaning need not happen. Preachers need not be so frustrated that they are tempted to abandon either preaching or the ministry itself. Laymen can expect to have help in sorting out their meanings and be affirmed in their secular vocations. These results, however, call for cooperation between pulpit and pew. There will have to be a recognition that communication requires partnership between communicators. Entirely new concepts of the role of the preacher and the role of the congregation will also have to be formed. The following chapters provide a guide to the formation of these new concepts and their application to the relation of the gospel to secular life.

2

THE LOSS OF MEANING

During the past ten years the faculty of the Institute for Advanced Pastoral Studies has devoted much study to the communication impasse that exists within the church and between the church and the world. We have found that communication in the church is both a major frustration and a primary area of need; and that high on the list of sources of communication-frustration is preaching. As a result of these studies the author feels that something relevant may now be said about the crisis in preaching, as well as about the widespread frustration of both clergy and laity that the conversations reported in the previous chapter reflect.

One of the methods the Institute has used to diagnose this communication problem is the following. Conference clergy attend a local church on Sunday morning to worship and listen to the sermon. A group of twelve or more laymen, representing a cross-section of the membership of the local church, are also asked to attend and to remain for a postservice discussion. After the service the conferees from the Institute and the selected laymen from the local church adjourn to separate rooms to discuss the worship experience and the sermon. To help structure these discussions each group is asked to consider such questions as these:

1. What did the preacher say to you? (The question is not: What did the preacher say?)
2. What difference, if any, do you think the message you heard will make to you in your relationships?
3. In what ways did the preacher's method, language, illustrations, and delivery help or hinder your hearing of his message?
4. What relation did you see between the worship and the preaching?
5. Did you help the preacher preach his sermon? Explain.

The laymen's discussion is taped in order that the conferees may listen to it and hear what the laymen think in comparison with their own reactions. Later in the day the conferees and the laymen meet together to discuss with each other their respective responses to the service and the sermon. Out of these discussions have come the statements about preaching which this chapter will consider.

The attitude of ministers toward preaching is mixed. On the one hand, they love preaching and return to it again and again with enthusiasm. On the other hand, they tend to be discouraged about its results as the conversation of the young clergymen in the first chapter dramatized. Some ministers work hard on their sermons; others only worry and procrastinate about preparation. All are dismayed at how little they are understood, how confused the people's responses are, and how irrelevant their sermons seem to be. They are baffled by the glazed, bewildered look that they often see in the eyes of their hearers as they deliver their message. The comments preachers hear after the service too often tell them that they were not understood. They frequently feel that they have worked out a good illustration or simile, only to discover that the congregation did not understand it. Some are dismayed at how secularized people are, how seldom biblical concepts and language are understood, and how rarely sermons seem to be able to touch the living reality of people's lives.

Disabling Images

Discussion with these ministers and many laymen has revealed that part of the difficulty seems to be the images that both have of the preacher and of preaching. These images stifle especially the efforts of ministers. They approach their task, sometimes consciously but mostly unconsciously, with the model of some great preacher in the back of their minds. Many of them have attempted to use in their own sermons the preaching methods of some of the famous preachers, but without profit to themselves or their people. As one minister said, "I wish I could find some way to be my own kind of preacher, even the kind that God might want me to be, rather than trying to be a preacher that fits the image someone else has given me." Similarly, young preachers often measure their sermons by standards derived from the great sermons which they studied in courses on preaching. Such comparisons have intimidating effects on them and cause them to be frustrated imitators, instead of being creative in their own way.

Another disabling image that both entertain is the image of the preacher as a performer who has to appear at least once a week, forty-eight times a year, and produce a masterpiece of communication. No artist in any other field is faced with such a demand. It is an impossible one, and many men feel the terrible burden of it. Under the influence of this image of the preacher as performer, the sermon becomes simply a performance and the congregation becomes an audience. The sermon as performance makes the Word aloof from the concerns of men and is unmet by the meanings of their lives. Its thought is exhibited but not participated in. Thus the performing word is a lonely word. One young preacher said, "I sometimes feel that when I am in the pulpit I am all alone, that no one is hearing me, and that no one cares that I am not heard. They want me to keep talking for the sake of appearances, but they do not want to hear."

On the other hand, the congregation that has been reduced to the state of an audience at a performance tends to become critical, passive, or irresponsible. They expect to be inspired, entertained, or to have their thinking done for them. In the last case, they tend to reject the thinking if they are in any way disturbed by what is said or by other concerns that compete for their attention.

The performer image of the preacher produces at least two responses in preachers that have a disastrous effect on their preaching of the gospel. One is a response of *exhibitionism,* which seeks to exploit the preaching situation; and the other is a response of *paralysis* that renders the effort of the preacher more and more impotent and ineffective.

The exhibitionist says that if preaching is a performance, let's make it a good one—and his performance becomes an end in itself. He exploits his talents; he exploits the needs of his people; he exploits the drama of the hu-

man situation; he exploits the dramatic qualities of the
gospel. Everything is said and done for the wrong reasons. Of course, there is a place for the dramatic and for
good acting when a preacher makes his use of the dramatic
as part of his offering to God and his people.

The second and more disabling response to the performer image is one of paralysis. In this case ministers are
so frightened by the demands preaching makes on them
that it is hard for them to get down to effective preparation for it. One of the things that I have discovered at the
Institute is how many ministers really cannot produce
anything for minimum presentation until the late hours
of Saturday or early Sunday morning. They may have
conscientiously begun their preparation on the previous
Monday, yet on Sunday morning, exhausted, anxious, and
full of self-disgust, they finally crawl into their pulpits
to deliver a sermon poorly focused, inadequately expressed, and unrelated to anything but the preacher's
desperation. They are like bakers who have mixed the
ingredients for bread, worked it into the shape of a
loaf, but are forced to deliver the bread before it is
baked because the customers have arrived and demand
immediate delivery. Under these circumstances the homiletical loaf is either unbaked or half baked. I do not say
this harshly or unkindly. The anxieties provoked by the
loneliness and demands of preaching can so paralyze
preachers' efforts that they cannot assemble their thoughts
in time to assimilate them and relate them to the contemporary context out of which they have to be heard.

The theology of ministry implicit in this kind of preaching, in which the preacher sees himself as solely responsible, contradicts the doctrine of ministry that we profess.
We profess that all ministries are the ministry of the
church. Since the church is made up of clergy *and* laity,

it follows that both have responsibilities in all ministries, and this is no less true for preaching. It is my belief that some of the weakness of preaching stems from the fact that it has been thoroughly clericalized and made the exclusive responsibility of the ordained minister. The alternative to the clericalization of preaching is the recovery of preaching as exemplified in our Lord's preaching. He preached for the most part in response to the needs and questions of people. He made use of what people already knew and understood, and employed symbols already familiar to them, such as seeds and sowers, sheep and shepherd, vineyard and wine. The loss of meaning to contemporary man of biblical and theological language, and the problems resulting from the accelerated process of secularization and technological advance, present special problems to contemporary preachers that make the recovery of our Lord's kind of preaching more than ever imperative. It is increasingly obvious that a traditionally oriented preacher will stand helpless in the face of a world which less and less needs either God as a working hypothesis or the rites and ceremonies that are traditionally associated with him.

3

LAYMEN'S RESPONSES
TO PREACHING

When we turn to laymen and ask them for their response to the preaching to which they listen, we hear comments that underline the seriousness of the problem but also give us clues to changes that the church might need to make. The comments that we shall quote have been taken from the hundreds of tapes we have at the Institute of laymen's discussions of sermons following services of worship.

The General Structure and
Content of Sermons

First, they complain almost unanimously that *sermons often contain too many ideas* and that these come at them too fast and are so complex that it is impossible to hold these ideas in mind long enough to relate them to the meaning of their lives. A point that the preacher is making may catch their attention, but while they are responding to it, he moves on so rapidly to other points that they lose the thread of his thought. What happens next is that they usually wander back mentally to their private preoccupations with life and work. Some of these laymen question whether the communication of a set of ideas is the purpose of a sermon at all. Incidentally, it improves laymen's listening and clergy's preaching to invite laymen's discussions with the clergy on the purpose of a sermon: Why do ministers preach? and, Why do laymen listen?

Laymen want simple sermons that teach deep truths. As one man said, "I like sermons to meet me where I live. I want to know how what I am excited about fits into the scheme of things; I want the sermon to build a fire under me that will burn all week." Adults frequently say the sermons they really like are those prepared and delivered to children because they are simple, vivid, employ ordinary language, and are concerned about life. They find themselves thinking about these sermons for weeks afterward, whereas, come Sunday evening they cannot even remember the sermon that was prepared for and delivered to them in the morning.

Second, laymen say sermons have *too much analysis and too little answer.* "We get analysis everywhere, but no answer from anyone. We think we should get it from the church." "Why do you give eighteen minutes to an analysis of man's need for the gospel and only two minutes on the gospel in relation to the need?" Some ask, "Don't you preachers really have a message? If so, why don't you preach it?" Indeed, the impression that many laymen have is that the only message preachers have is the one of what is wrong with the world, with the result that they are left wondering what the "Good News" is, if any, in relation to the analysis.

"Another thing I don't like about some preaching," said

another layman who speaks for the growing number of
his kind, "is that preachers are always on the defensive.
Even their analysis of life is tilted in favor of the church
and religion." Another said, "Your defensiveness for God,
church, and religion makes me wonder what's wrong with
them that they need your protection. Why don't you act
as if you trusted what you say you believe in and state it
and use it less qualifyingly and more daringly?"

Third, another common comment from laymen states
that *sermons are too formal and impersonal.* The lack of
personal urgency in preaching conveys the impression that
the minister is not dealing with life-and-death issues.
These doubts cause laymen to raise questions about methods of delivery. They seem to sense that there ought to
be a difference between a lecture and a sermon. "I don't
see why anyone who spends as much time as a minister
does in public speaking has to confine himself to a writ-
ten sermon. He can write it if he has to, but he ought not
to have to read it!" Another person reported, "I have often
wondered if preachers are trying so hard to be correct and
orthodox that they are afraid they won't be forgiven if they
speak out of their honest or even heated convictions." Or
again, "I wish he would say what he feels." They are of
the opinion that some sense of linguistic urgency on the
part of the speaker suggests that he himself has wrestled
with the truth he is presenting which, they think, adds
to a sense of authenticity. Apparently there is a longing
on the part of laymen for the preacher to give an honest,
intelligent, passionate, personal presentation of Christian
conviction rather than the coldly rational, dispassionate
presentation of objective truth.

Laymen also make comments which show that they feel
the need of more direct address in preaching and less
talking *about* the faith as if it were only a set of optional

ideas. I judge that what they are really looking for in preaching is more "I-Thou" quality.*

Ideas, Terms, and Illustrations Used in Sermons

Fourth, laymen feel that *preachers assume that laymen have a greater knowledge and understanding of biblical and theological lore and language than they actually do.* As a result of this assumption preachers fail to explain or elaborate various vital ideas they present and laymen simply fail to grasp the point of these sermons. One man said, "If I used that much jargon with my customers I would lose them." They complain that many of the words and concepts used in preaching are meaningless to them. When asked what some of these words were, they mentioned "salvation," "judgment," "redemption," "gospel," and so on. These are not terms by which laymen today either convey or receive meaning. When preachers use these words and concepts without really explaining them, the words and concepts cease to be effective symbols of communication. Another part of the difficulty comes from the minister's failure to explain the nature and purpose of symbols and myths. Without such explanation laymen have no choice but to interpret the symbol or myth literally, and of course it then seems senseless to them in the context of contemporary life.

The concept of myth, for example, is a source of confusion. Because clergy will not take the trouble to instruct

* For an excellent application of that principle to the theme we are discussing, I refer the reader to Herbert Farmer's *Servant of the Word* (Philadelphia: Fortress Press, 1964; paperback).

laymen precisely in the meanings of concepts, many people think that a myth represents something that is not true. They have not been helped to understand that a myth is a story which represents a truth. When the preacher says to some people, therefore, that the creation story is a myth, they become angry or bewildered because they think he is saying that God did not create the world. When he explains to them, however, that the story (myth) does affirm belief that God created the "heavens and earth and all that in them is," but does not require belief that he did it in six twenty-four-hour days, they are set free to correlate their religious beliefs with their scientific knowledge.

Laymen need help also in distinguishing between a word or myth and the meaning or truth they represent. The word "God" and the being of God are not synonymous, of course, but in their discussions many people seem to equate them. To use an analogy, we need to distinguish between the contents of a package and the package. The creation story in Genesis is, for example, the package containing the belief about the origin of the universe. Lay people are responsive to and appreciative of such distinctions, and of the assistance they receive from them for their thinking.

Preaching also suffers from the failure to provide opportunities for the laity to wrestle with biblical and theological concepts in the context of their own lives and in their own terms. A notable result of this is the prevalence among church people of moralism and the absence of a sense of dependence on forgiveness. True, most preachers preach "grace," but the people seem to hear "law." The good news of their being accepted in spite of their guilt never reaches the laity and, as a result, they become mired in the processes of self-justification with its attendant moralism and self-righteousness. One corrective of this condition would be to preach grace but provide people with opportunity and guidance to understand its meaning in secular and nontheological terms, that is, in their own terms.

Our study agrees with that of William D. Thompson,* who has demonstrated that the minister tends to idealize his congregation and to assume more knowledge on their part than they actually possess. In his words, "communication between pulpit and pew may sometimes fail because ministers assume greater sophistication for their audiences than the facts warrant."

Fifth, many laymen complain that *sermons are too propositional; they contain too few illustrations;* and *the illustrations are often too literary and not helpful.* They would like ministers to use more illustrations from life, the kind of illustration that would really "light up" for them aspects of their everyday lives. One vivacious and intelligent woman said, "I get bored with the unimaginative presentation of so many strange thoughts." Someone else said, "The sermons which get my attention are the ones in which they relate a story of everyday living and use it to tell us about Christian living." Still another person reports that his attention is often caught by something that is familiar to him, and he wishes that ministers would use situations and issues that are common to their own lives as a resource in presenting new truth. They suggest that preachers are too preoccupied with the past, with theories of life, and with the traditional. This comment, interestingly enough, is the other side of the one com-

* *Listener's Guide to Preaching* (Nashville, Tenn.: Abingdon Press, 1966).

monly made by preachers that their main source of supply for preaching comes from their books and seminary notes. One layman, when referring to biblical allusions and illustrations, said, "I'm sick and tired of being talked to as if I were a Corinthian."

Secularized, urbanized, technological people are not helped by biblical, pastoral, and rural references and illustrations. Efforts must be made to find contemporary symbols for timeless meanings so that there may be a meeting of meaning between contemporary man and the eternal God.

Finally, these laymen report that *too many sermons simply reach a dead end and give no guidance to commitment and action.* This kind of preaching, laymen feel, goes nowhere and relates to nothing in life. Here are some comments: "You talk about love as if there were no people hating each other." "You talk about justice as if the world wasn't tearing itself apart." "It's all very well to tell us that God is love, but what does that mean to me, living as I do in the tangle of hostility which is a part of my work?" "Sometimes," commented another layman, "after I have heard a sermon I feel like asking, 'So what?' "

But the most telling criticism of the dead-end nature of preaching was that expressed by the man who said, "You preachers seem concerned only about the sick, poor, and weak, as if God were a substitute for adequacy. What do you have to say to the strong men, the powerful, the influencers of our culture? I don't think we really need the kind of God you talk about."

In sum, our examination of conventional preaching and its results has revealed that the intended content of sermons is poorly communicated. By actual count, less than one third of the people who attended the postservice discussion were able to make a clear statement of the sermon's central question and the "answer" that it offered. This fact in itself places upon the church a heavy responsibility to review the preaching-communication problem and to take the necessary steps to solve it.

4

MOVING FROM FRUSTRATION

In addition to findings on conventional preaching presented in the preceding chapter, there are other observations about conventional preaching to be made and findings to be considered that are important to our discussion.

Conventional preaching, we have seen, is largely "one way" or monological in its concept of communication. It has become locked up in a stereotype that stifles the potential creativity of every preacher. This "performer" image of preaching, which is the name of the stereotype, throttles the potential power of preaching. The purpose of communication is to produce a meeting of meaning from two sides. Monologue, however, is concerned only with the imposition of meaning from one side. The monologist or "performer" does not see or hear; he only talks. And the more frustrated and anxious he becomes about his communication, the more he talks and the less he sees and hears. In fact, it comes close to the truth to say that the monological preacher believes that he has the Word and that God speaks only through him.

The idea of preaching as monological also receives expression or confirmation in the very arrangements for preaching and in the presentation of content and the manner of its delivery, with a complete lack of provision for feedback.

The Characteristics of Conventional Preaching

First, let us look at the physical arrangements for preaching: the pulpit is elevated; the preacher looks down; the people look up. Often, as the lights in the church are turned down and a spotlight turned on the preacher, the congregation disappears into an identity-hiding gloom. The elevation of the pulpit lifts the Word of God above life, and would seem to contradict the concept of its embodiment in the life of the people. The arrangement, moreover, confirms the stereotype of the relation between clergy and laity in which the Word is removed from the people and made the preacher's exclusive sphere of responsibility.

Second, the manner of preaching reflects the clergy's monopolistic role. The preacher speaks, the people listen. He is active, they are passive. The preaching is usually didactic and impersonal. The power of the Word is often weakened because there is little struggle to find its meaning for men today. The concern of much preaching does not seem to extend beyond the walls of the church, or the preoccupations of institution. There are too many preachers who seem unaware that men are searching for meaning, asking questions, or involved in life-and-death struggles. They preach to give meaning to people, but are oblivious of the meanings people have already.

Third, the content of preaching, I am afraid, demonstrates an unrelatedness of the gospel to life which has

been acquired by the preacher in an academic study of
Christianity. In much of it the Good News of the New
Creation in Christ seems to have been reduced to the di-
mensions of the practices of a cult. Preachers seem to be
unaware that for many in the congregation, to say nothing of people who no longer go to church, the formulations of belief and interpretation of Christianity seem to
be obsolete. Growing numbers of church people, too, are
thoroughly secularized and find their meanings in a technological pragmatic society, and, while continuing to observe the traditional expressions of worship, teaching, and
sacraments, these people find their search for meaning
more and more unmet by the church's teaching.

A fourth characteristic of conventional preaching is seen
in the absence of organized response or feedback from the
congregation. Lack of feedback strengthens all the stereotypes which people entertain about preaching. Preaching
is frequently done to an invisible congregation because
the lights have been turned down; yet the facial expressions and bodily postures and movements of the congregation are communications in response to the preacher,
and he needs to see and note them as at least partial
guidance for his speaking. The custom of preaching without response from the congregation is irresponsible communication and endangers, more than anything else, the
preacher's relevance. Science and industry have made phe-
nomenal progress because they uniformly check and study
the results of anything they do with the intention of
changing production in the light of what has been learned.
That kind of disciplined operation is not prevalent in the
church. Even in this day when clergymen are raising questions about the effectiveness of their ministry, they commonly fail to test for obsolescence or effectiveness. Too
many clergy are self-protective. They are afraid of honest

evaluation and inclined to receive criticism not as a source of learning but as a source of personal rejection. The attitude of many clergy is expressed in the statement of one of them: "I would like to benefit from comments of my congregation, but I'm afraid of their criticism." Such ministers obviously do not hold themselves to the same kind of rigorous discipline and judgment as do laymen in their fields of endeavor.

Another reason why this lack of feedback is serious is that it removes the clergyman and the church from many of the possibilities of correction and renewal. The minister is fond of saying that God speaks to the church through the world, but how is the Word of God going to be available to the clergy if they do not listen to anybody through whom God might speak? They need to remember that the laity are the ones in whom the meanings of the gospel and the meanings of the world meet. If they do not listen to the laity, they cannot learn much about the meeting of these meanings. All clergymen, no matter what kind of ministry they are carrying on, need to ask themselves what kind of built-in feedback they have in their operation.

The prevalence of this performer-monologue stereotype of preaching among the clergy is confirmed in the responses of ministers to the question: How much time do you spend on your sermons and what resources do you regularly use?

Preparing to Preach

Their response to the first part of the question is often one of embarrassment, because the amount of time that they spend in preparation is so little. The reasons for this

are mainly two: (1) the pressure of other duties makes
it difficult for ministers to stake out and hold time for
study; (2) their frustrations in preaching increase their
ambivalence about it, and, therefore, their likelihood to
procrastinate. Their answers also indicate that preparation for preaching is understood only as the time spent
in their study reading books.

Their response to the second part of the question reveals that most preachers think of the resources available
to them mainly in terms of Bible commentaries, books on
the theme under consideration, and notes from the courses
that they had in seminary. Their relationships and experiences with people and their reflections upon these are
not consciously explored and used as resources. Ministers
are not trained to reflect upon human action and events,
to interpret them theologically, and to regard such reflection as important as the study of books. Preparation for
preaching, therefore, should include time spent studying
the human and social implications of their pastoral and
community relationships; reading papers and magazines;
listening to radio; watching television; attending the
theater and movies in order that the church's preaching
may engage the meanings that influence people with the
meanings of the gospel.

Moreover, preachers admit that they fail to make use of
significant events in the lives of their people and ignore
their meaning instead of making them a part of the curriculum of Christian teaching by affirming, complement-
ing, and evaluating them. Inquiries reveal that preachers
do not pay attention to people's responses to movies, television programs, and other provocative events in the life
of the community and its people. They do not ask, "What
meanings have these events produced in the minds of peo-

ple? What is the relation of these meanings to the gospel? What meanings can be affirmed? Which ones need to be challenged, corrected or complemented?" One minister told of seeing *Who's Afraid of Virginia Woolf* and added that he did not like it. When asked what responses the movie elicited in his people, he had to acknowledge that he did not know. Their response to the movie and the meaning they brought out of it were potentially available to the minister's preaching, but he was oblivious of them, and to that extent he had to preach blind.

It thus seems clear that the difficulty with conventional preaching stems from an inadequate concept of communication, and that no amount of homiletical instruction will improve matters until that instruction is based on a true principle of communication. Most preachers want to be relevant and helpful to their people, but they do not know, for the most part, how to be. The majority of congregations tend in their evaluations to rate their ministers highly on their over-all ministry, but much less highly on their sermons.

Research reveals that although ministers are seen as concerned with the needs of the laity, they are not commonly perceived as "actively seeking or desiring, nor receptive to their views on, or contribution to, the sermon." Two thirds of the people regularly attending church seldom or never indicated to the minister any kind of response to his preaching. While the majority in many congregations accept monological, authoritarian preaching as ideal, there is a growing, vigorous minority who would welcome the opportunity for interaction. Several of the young people whose conversation was recorded in the first chapter expressed their desire for a chance to react out of their concerns to the church's preaching.

Is Preaching Obsolescent?

In view of the negative findings we have been presenting, we must now consider whether preaching is obsoles-
cent, a charge made by some critics. Before answering this
question, we shall grant that changing life requires change
in the forms for meeting life and that we may well expect
the form of the church's ministry to change if the truth
is to be served and the meanings of life are to be met.
On the other hand, we ought not to forget that obsolescence may be caused by incomplete and inefficient use of
things rather than by their "dated" nature. Therefore,
before we agree with the criticism and abandon preaching, we ought to test to see how well all the potential resources of preaching are being used.

The waning influence of the church has frequently been
cited as evidence of the ineffectiveness of preaching. The
monological, "performer" stereotype of conventional
preaching, as we have seen, frustrates the clergy, impov-
erishes the laity, and fails to engage men who are living
on the frontier of human thought and action.

Many clergymen who have listened to the laymen's comments on our tapes are surprised by the acuteness of their
perceptions. They admit that the criticisms of the laymen
are both just and perceptive. They realize that they have
not been trained to communicate with laymen. One spoke
for many when he said, "I think I was better prepared to
be a professor of theology than a preacher to businessmen."
Another said that because his seminary training was so
inadequate he had never been more than a communications amateur. As a theological educator it has often
seemed to me that we do rather successfully educate fu-

ture ministers away from the possibility of communicating with those to whom they are sent. Here is a matter that calls for corrective action.

Preaching is meant to be communication. Communication is necessary to relationship, and without it there can be no relation. The great purpose of preaching is not that the congregation shall hear the preacher, but that the dialogue between God and man be directed and informed. Preaching, therefore, is significant only when it is communication that activates and informs the dialogue between God and man. The preacher is important as the educated and skilled agent of that dialogue. His formulations are important when they stimulate people's formulations of the meaning of their contemporary experience with man and God.

The church has always placed communication with its members and the world at large as a main task. Throughout its history it has used a variety of means to accomplish this—preaching, teaching, music, and all the visual resources of art and architecture. From the beginning, however, the most widely used verbal means of communication in the gathered church has been the sermon. But preaching and the sermon have been thought of as the exclusive work of the clergy, and the laity has been assigned the role of passive consumer rather than active participant. In fact, theological education pays little attention in courses on preaching to communication and the principles of communication as such. A knowledge of the process of communication is assumed, and teachers then proceed to present and analyze different kinds of sermons, their structure and delivery. Furthermore, practice preaching is usually made to an audience of classmates and instructors, a most atypical congregation and one that the student may never again face in his career.

Meeting the Communication Problem

The contemporary problem of preaching is largely a communication problem. Some critics think that the problem is that men do not have anything to communicate and, therefore, that the answer is to increase a more disciplined study of Bible and theology. On the contrary, ministers already have more content than they can communicate, and if added stress was put on the subject matter of theological learning without adequate training in communication, the situation of the minister would be worse. Preaching is more than a process of transmitting ideas about Christian creed, cult, and conduct with the expectation that these ideas will be understood, accepted, and translated into action. Preaching that is concerned only with the transmission of ideas fails to communicate and convey to men the meaning of God's action in Christ. Preaching is an encounter involving not only content but relationship, not only ideas but action, not only logic but emotion, not only understanding but commitment.

The emerging science of communication has developed a critical evaluation of preaching that allows us to diagnose the real problem and, further, has provided us with resources that may be used to solve the problem. Until ten years ago most studies on preaching were concerned with the role of the preacher. Current studies from within the church address themselves to the role of the congregation as active participants in the church's preaching. These studies have grown out of recent research that establishes communication as a two-way or transactional process.

Both experimentation and communication theory stress, then, the importance of active lay participation in preaching. The reasons for this we shall now enumerate and examine.

Why should laymen be involved in the church's preaching?

First, they should be participants because they are a part of the church, a part of the people of God! As such they are not meant to be passive recipients of, but active participants in, the witness of the church in the world.

Second, they should participate because, out of the data and experiences of their lives, they produce insights and points of view that must be taken into account if there is to be a true meeting of meaning between man and God.

Third, they should be participants because it is Christian belief that God speaks to men through men, especially through his people if they are open to him. If communication is two-way, then preaching should mean: (1) communication between congregation and preacher; and (2) between members of the congregation and people with whom they live and work. All of this transaction is part of the total act of preaching and has an important bearing upon our understanding of what a sermon is.

This point is particularly important and relevant because of man's enormously increasing knowledge, the meaning of which has to be correlated with the meaning of the gospel. Ordained ministers cannot make this correlation by themselves because their knowledge and training is limited. Ministers must realize that in the task of correlation they are inescapably dependent on the laity. They must learn to accept a communication process in which the laity actively feed into the preaching of the gospel the data and insights of their lives so that the contemporary and the traditional heritage will meet. Thus, tradition will be renewed through dialogue with the contemporary; and the contemporary will be given depth and perspective through dialogue with the tradition. The relation between the contemporary and the traditional may be represented by the following diagram.

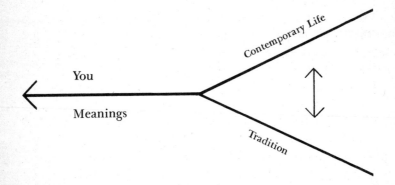

This dialogue between the meanings of the contemporary and tradition needs to occur in every individual's life. If a person keeps them separate, his sense of values will be fragmented and his concepts disorganized. The churches are filled with people who religiously live out a tradition that is unchallenged and unrenewed. They are traditionalists, advocates of a status quo, opposed to change, and holding exclusionist attitudes toward anything new. There are also people who are only contemporary in their interest and who scoff at tradition. They are proud that their concepts are very modern but they are superficial and transitory because they lack rootage in a historical context. But the person who maintains dialogue between the historical and the contemporary has relevance and perspective, and the meanings with which he meets life will be a product of the dialogue. He will have both strength, resulting from tested convictions, and daring, because of a sense of security in relation to the possibilities of life.

The culture also needs to engage in the same dialogue between the tradition that produced it and the contemporary meanings of its life. Each generation must not only accept its heritage but also engage it with the best of its contemporary meanings. Whenever a generation fails to maintain such dialogue the tradition lose₎ its vitality. When each age engages its tradition in honest and vigorous dialogue, the tradition grows in vitality and greatness. Our present age is exciting because there is a rich exchange between tradition and the contemporary in many fields. On the contrary, much church life, as it is lived on the local level, reveals a fear and caution that keeps "religious" meanings separated from contemporary questions and affirmations.

The church's preaching has this engagement between the traditional and the contemporary as its task. The church preaches the Word of God in order that life may realize its meaning and promise; and the church preaches in order that the Word of God may be recognized by man out of his meanings as the true word for him to which he may respond with trust.

The crisis of preaching, therefore, exists because the meanings of the gospel are unmet by the meanings we bring out of our lives; and the meanings that emerge out of living are unmet by the timeless meanings of God's Word for us. The performer, monological, clergy-monopolized type of preaching is incapable of meeting the crisis constructively.

Obviously, a change is needed. We shall now consider what kind of change this must be.

5

THE PREACHING SITUATION

The purpose of preaching is to cause the Word of God to take flesh in the lives of men and women. When the word indwells us, we as individual Christians, and as Christians in a corporate group, may without effrontery say, "We are the message." But for preaching to be this kind of communication, it must have the quality of dialogue, otherwise it *will* be arrogant and untrustworthy, or remain simply a statement abstracted from life.

Dialogue is the interaction between two or more people in response to the truth; it is also the process of assimilation by which perceived truth becomes embodied in the person, becomes part of him. As we see it, dialogue provides the give and take, check and balance, test and correction, that human beings need both to understand rightly and to communicate accurately.

In *Miracle of Dialogue* we defined dialogue in these words:

Dialogue is that address and response between persons in which there is a flow of meaning between them in spite of all the obstacles that normally would block the relationship. It is that interaction between persons in which one of them seeks to give himself as he is to the other, and seeks also to know the other as the other is. This means that he will not attempt to impose his own truth and view on the other. Such is the relationship which characterizes dialogue and is the precondition to dialogical communication.*

If the dialogical process is to be an indispensable part of preaching, it will require of preacher and people that they participate as partners in order to ensure a meeting of meaning from both sides.

Here it is in order to differentiate carefully between method and principle. By *method* we mean the way the communication is delivered: in monologue, for example, one person addresses another; in dialogue two people exchange communication. By *principle* we mean the whole concern that governs the communication: when the monological principle is employed, one person tells another what he ought to know, and the communication is content-centered; when the dialogical principle governs a communication, the speaker feels responsible for and responds to the patterns of experience and understanding that his listener brings to the situation, and thus the listener is encouraged to grapple with his own meaning in relation to the speaker's meaning.

When we make this distinction between method and principle, we can readily see that a communication which in terms of method is monologue (one speaker) may at the same time be governed by the principle of dialogue; and similarly, although two people may be addressing each other, if neither is responsible for or responsive to the meanings of the other, the communication is dialogue only in terms of method and lacks the dialogical principle.

What do these simple observations mean for preaching, which is so obviously monologue in terms of method—

* Reuel L. Howe, *The Miracle of Dialogue* (New York, 1963; paperback, 1964).

that is, only one person speaks. They mean that the crucial point in relation to the sermon is the principle the preacher employs—how he speaks. If he employs the dialogical principle, dialogue is implicit in his preparation, his delivery, and in the content of his sermon.

The listener too will quickly recognize the presence of this dialogical principle. For he finds it hard to respond to the thoroughly monological address, where the speaker seems preoccupied and not interested in the listener, and the subject merely static content.

On the other hand, when addressed dialogically, the listener knows that *he* is being addressed by another, and that the content is living truth which speaks to meanings coming from his own experience. He experiences an invitation to participate even though at the moment he cannot speak aloud. But because he is addressed dialogically, he will speak and act later. Such is the power of the lecture or sermon, when it serves the dialogical principle of communication. The lecture or sermon then ceases to be simply monologue, and becomes in principle dialogue.

Let us apply these observations in detail to the preaching situation with the help of the diagram opposite.

1. *The Congregation.* The congregation is made up of men and women who are finite, sinful human beings, yet also endowed with unrealized creativity. They are products of both the tradition from which they come and the contemporary world of which they are a part. As we have seen, there is the question whether or not there has been in their lives a dialogue between the meanings of their contemporary living and the traditions which gave them their original values and concepts. They come to the homiletical event from their respective worlds and activities: their respective homes, industries, and profes-

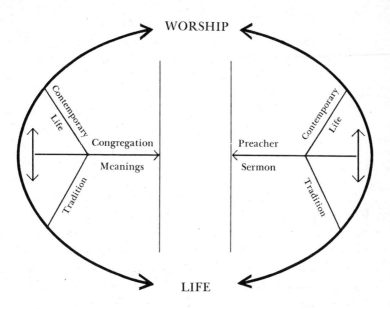

sions; their own type of work and inclination for recrea-
tion, their own degree and kind of social and civic life.
Out of their respective experiences, both traditional and
contemporary, and influenced by their education and their
vocational commitments, they bring to their listening,
consciously and unconsciously, meaning in the form of
questions, hypotheses, affirmations, doubts, fears, and so
on. These meanings are important to the preaching situation which we are analyzing in that they provide the potential for one side of the dialogue that must characterize
preaching if it is to communicate successfully. The question, then, is: Will these meanings from their respective
lives and experience be summoned by the congregation
to meet the meanings of the preacher; will these meanings
in turn be met by his meanings so that both preacher and
congregation are confronted anew and more deeply by the
meanings of the gospel?

The ministry of the congregation during the preacher's sermon is to listen, not passively, but actively out of their own meanings, and in their very listening to challenge and encourage the preacher in what he is trying to say. In contrast to this concept of the congregation's ministry stands the concept of its passive role, the concept usually governing the situation. On the basis of hundreds of conversations with laymen I have to report that laymen have no awareness of responsibility toward the sermon. Many laymen, for example, are puzzled by the question, "In what ways did you or might you have helped the preacher preach his sermon?" The question obviously suggests something that is inconceivable to them. Furthermore, not many, if any, laymen ever receive instruction from the church about the role of the congregation with respect to the preacher's sermon or how they are to listen to it.

Later I will have something to say about other parts of the congregation's ministry, such as preparation and delivery of the church's preaching.

2. *The Preacher.* A second part of the preaching situation is represented by the preacher. He, too, is a man, always finite and sinful, yet also with unrealized creative powers. He, too, is a product of some tradition, a representative of a denomination, and also of the age in which he is living. He has been professionally trained, as a rule, in the history, beliefs, and practices of the Christian church and in the Scriptures. He is both a man and an ordained trained minister. An important question here is: What is the relation between the man and the training that he has received? It is to be hoped that there is a correlation between what he is as a man and what he is as a minister. Otherwise, there is the danger that his

being a minister and a preacher may pre-empt his humanity (his being as man), in which case he cannot possibly be a free partner in the dialogue that preaching ought to be.

For the preaching occasion he prepares himself to address the congregation on a subject suggested by circumstance, or dictated by liturgical calendar, or selected by him for one or more reasons. He brings to the preparation of his address all that he has learned and can formulate out of his study of Scripture, his doctrinal understandings, and his knowledge of life. His task is to present his theme in fifteen, twenty, or twenty-five minutes in such a way that he engages the meanings of his hearers with the meanings of the gospel. His image of himself and his role in this exchange, it must be noted, are crucial for what may or may not happen in the course of the sermon encounter and in the lives of the people subsequently. If his image is of himself as a performer, if he conceives of himself as the informer and his congregation as passive recipients, if he thinks of himself as answer man, and fails to address himself to the questions and insights of the people, he will fail them and the gospel, too. If, on the other hand, he sees himself as the directing agent of an exchange between the meanings his people bring out of their lives and the meanings of the gospel, exciting meetings of meaning will occur that will profoundly affect both the people and the world in which they live.

In the actual preaching encounter much, then, will depend on how well both preacher and people have used their eyes and ears prior to the encounter. This may seem a strange comment to make about an activity that is conventionally and exclusively associated with verbal articulation. Preparatory to speaking, however, the preacher must use his eyes and ears. He must learn to see as well as to hear what his people are communicating and what the world in which they both live is communicating.

In his relationships with them and with the world he must frequently let the gospel be present incognito. He cannot live and wear it like a clerical collar. Instead of talking about the gospel to men who, for the most part, are unable to hear it in its traditional forms, he must learn to listen to people and observe them in a context that has no awareness of the gospel. That means that he listens and observes with respect for what he sees and hears, with compassion and tolerance, with humility for lessons that he can learn, with a readiness to change and even to die in the sense of relinquishing some cherished belief or practice without assurance that he will soon find anything better. The preacher today may at times have simply to live with the questions and problems of human life, aware that God *is* dead, certainly for many people, if not for him. The preacher today must turn away from easy answers, avoid addressing himself to questions people are not asking, and strive to recognize and understand the questions people are asking and the answers or clues for which they are searching. Today men are more interested in men than they are in God; and the questions they ask concern human relations more than divine relations. Yes, the first responsibility of the modern preacher is to listen and observe. For to talk about God before listening to the individual man and his questions is useless today.

There comes a time, however, for the minister to stop listening and to start talking because the man-question has been heard and understood and something needs to be said about God. In our effort to correct the monologue from the church to the world, let us not fall into the trap of substituting the monologue from the world to the church—that is, of offering it as the preacher's sermon.

Some preachers have become so man-oriented that they no longer speak about God. Dialogical preaching is the opposite of this. It is a two-way give-and-take; it is a partnership. In dialogical preaching we need the question *and* the answer. The question awaits the answer, and the answer needs the guidance of the question. The preacher is, so to speak, master-of-ceremonies in the dialogue between question and answer.

The responsibilities of the laity in this exchange are the same as those of the preacher. They, too, are to listen and observe as they live in order to discern the meaning of their experiences and to learn to formulate their questions and insights. The secrets and the powers of life become available to people who learn to live reflectively. They see meaning in the various issues that come up in their business and family life, in community relations, in civic and social responsibilities, even in leisure. People who live without discerning the meanings of their lives contribute little, if anything, to the preaching encounter: they bring little conscious meaning to it, they receive little in return—and there is nothing that a preacher can do in twenty minutes to change the situation. An unreflective and, therefore, unprepared people can have as disastrous effect on a preaching encounter as an unprepared preacher, because they are not able to take their part in the church's preaching.

People like Jack and Janet Spread and Fred and Beth Stickman would bring much to a preaching encounter if their partner, the preacher, could accept and build on their questions and their search. One reason for nurturing a dialogical relationship between pulpit and pew is that in the process people will bring more and more meanings out of their lives to bear on what they hear. The more they hear, the more reflectively they are able to live; and thus the more they will bring to the encounter both in the world and in their gatherings at church.

3. *Worship.* A third part of the preaching situation is worship. It is the context for the dialogue between man and God which is the primary concern of preaching. What is the relation between preaching and worship? Is preaching a part of worship, or is worship a prelude to preaching? What concept of worship in relation to preaching exists in the minds of the preacher and of the congregation? If preaching is a dialogue between the Word of God and the word of man, and worship is dialogue between the relationship with God and the relationship with man, then it should follow that preaching has to have a contextual relationship in worship. What is that contextual relationship, and how can it be realized both in worship and in preaching? I raise these questions because my observations suggest that there is little realized relationship between preaching and worship.

Our research has shown that 50 per cent of the people questioned thought the sermon was the most meaningful part of the service. They regarded the worship itself as simply a prelude to the preaching. Some even admitted to a sense of relief when the "preliminaries are out of the way so we can get down to the real business of listening to what the preacher has prepared for us."

Few church people were able to identify much connection between the service and the sermon, which leads one to believe that few ministers plan the service and sermon to be two complementary aspects of one experience.

Here is an area that awaits to be enriched jointly by liturgical renewal and church renewal. Preaching needs the dialogue of give-and-take in worship just as worship needs the give-and-take between the Word of God and the word of man.

What else does a man have to give God than the offering of himself with all of the meanings of his life that he can marshal? And with what else can he hear the Word of God than with those very meanings that are the distillations of his own responsible thought and feeling? If there is no offering of one's self and life in worship, there can be no real speaking and hearing in preaching.

An illustration may help to make this point clear. A young lawyer, during a discussion, admitted having a troubled conscience because he was employed by a bank to represent them in a foreclosure proceeding in which there was deliberate withholding of information that prejudiced the issue. He had failed to correct the matter with those who were in charge of the case, and as a result was deeply troubled. He kept trying to justify himself by thinking that, since he was employed by the bank, he had to do what they required of him, but he continued to feel guilty.

The discussion group of which he was a part had begun the day's program with a communion service. A general confession was a part of the service and he was asked whether he had confessed his part in the foreclosure matter. He replied, "No." Then he was asked, "What content from your life did you have for confession?" and he admitted that at the time he had not thought of anything. Here we have an example of a very common separation of life from worship. Because of the separation the young lawyer had no basis for hearing and understanding the preaching of the gospel of forgiveness and justification "by faith through grace." We must help people close the gap between life and worship in order that preaching may have an enabling context. Worship that is rooted in the meanings of life opens the person through the act of offering and thanksgiving to the possibility of dialogue between himself and God.

6

BARRIERS TO

DIALOGICAL PREACHING

In the preceding chapter we considered three parts of the preaching situation: the congregation, the preacher, and the life-worship dialogue as the context for preaching. We shall now consider a fourth factor: the presence of meaning barriers.

Most of us assume the process of communication to be easier than it actually is: namely, that if we will tell people what they need to know, and if they will have the good grace to hear and do what we tell them, the job will be done. Nothing could be more mistaken than that expectation, as the young clergymen whose conversation was recorded in the opening chapter discovered.

Aside from the difficulty of saying what we mean, the real question is whether we will be heard and heeded. There are some inevitable complications that need to be considered: the barriers to communication that exist in every relationship, including that of preacher and congregation, as represented in the diagram on the following page.

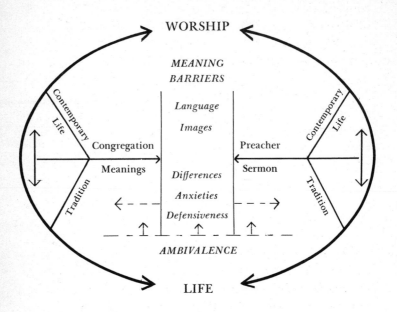

The Nature of the Barriers

A barrier is a block that prevents a meeting of meaning between two or more people. In the case of preaching the barriers are usually between the preacher and his consciously organized effort to communicate a message, and the individual persons who make up his congregation. As we have already pointed out (and as the arrows in the diagram indicate), there is a movement of meaning from each side; but the arrows moving in the opposite direction indicate that meanings often do not meet and return without receiving response. It is as if the meanings hit something between the communicators that caused them to bounce back.

These barriers exist in and between both preacher and

congregation. Fundamental to all barriers is the condition of general ambivalence that all human beings—and specifically, here, preacher and congregation—experience in communication: that is, as human beings, we both want to speak and do not want to, and we both want to hear and are afraid to do so. Such ambivalence stems from our ontological condition—that is, we both want to know and be known, and do not want to know and be known —and, therefore, our power to represent ourselves and to hear the representation of others is adversely affected. Concretely, this means that the preacher, as he stands in his pulpit, both wants to speak and preach the gospel and does not want to; and his people, as they sit before him, have come to hear, yet do not want to hear the gospel.

There are many illustrations of how this ambivalence affects us. The preacher can be ambivalent about preaching the gospel itself because to truly present it truly brings him under judgment and calls him to commitments that threaten his way of life. And members of the congregation experience the same kind of ambivalence. They would like to respond to the promise of renewal that they sense in the Good News, but they also want to hold back a great part of themselves because of the demand for change in them that comes with the promise. And thus each occasion of preaching is marked by an ambivalence on both sides.

Part of the preaching task is to overcome this ambivalence, and it can be done only as both preacher and people accept the ambivalence and help each other with it. In contrast to this realistic aim, I find that both preacher and congregation are often unaware of any ambivalence in themselves and each other and, therefore, cannot help each other toward removing its disabling effect.

Sharing the Problem

They could help each other by at least sharing the problem. The church's preachers and teachers for the most part seem to ignore the processes of interaction and learning. What goes on between preacher and congregation is rarely talked about, identified, and made a part of the curriculum—that is, made a source of learning. Neglect of this part of the preaching encounter centers all meaning of preaching on content which, because it lacks correlation with its human counterpart, cannot possibly seem important or challenging. What happens when a preacher identifies and discusses his own and his congregation's ambivalence about honest communication and about the gospel? Most people welcome the preacher's effort. They like his honesty, and it engenders trust of him. They pay more attention to the other things that he says. They become less guarded in meeting his message with their own meanings. They talk with each other and with people outside their own church circle about the experience they have had together and the ambivalence they see in all relationships. And they seem to acquire some power over it because they recognize and name the condition.

There will be some people, of course, who will resist and be alienated by such honesty between preacher and congregation, but their responses have to be accepted as inevitable.

Some Specific Barriers

This ambivalence is also reflected in certain other identifiable symptoms which act as more specific barriers to a meeting of meaning.

Jim Darling and his friends had found that language can be a major barrier. And yet how strange when language is supposed to be a carrier of meaning. Language can be both a barrier and a carrier. When people, for example, bring different meanings to the use of the same word, their communication gets hung up on that word. The same word also may have different meanings and that will make it difficult for participants in the communication to understand each other. One person understands "judgment," for example, to mean condemnation; another person may understand it to mean evaluation leading to reconstruction. Their communication may then be complicated or blocked by the different understandings they have of the meaning of the word.

We should remember, too, that the meaning a person has for a word is not only a matter of semantics. It may have its roots in life's experiences. Language problems are often expressions of relationship problems. The word "Bible," for example, can have a repressive moralistic meaning for one person because the Bible and its teaching was used to suppress gay and spontaneous responses during his childhood. Another person will have joyous and constructive meanings for the Bible because it was used to elicit responses of trust and love. Similarly "home" for one person is a place of fulfillment, for another a source of anxiety and dread, both meanings coming out of the relationships experienced in the home.

Another aspect of the language problem has to do with technical language which applies to preaching. Many biblical and theological terms, as we have already noted in other connections, are foreign and uncongenial to contemporary man. He neither receives nor conveys meaning by their use. Words and concepts such as "creation," "fall," "heaven," "hell," "kingdom," "resurrection," "ascension," "redemption" are meaningless to thousands of people, including lifelong church members. And yet the preacher has been trained to employ this language and is baffled to discover its ineffectiveness. The traditional words, however, need not be discarded, but when the preacher uses them, he should explain their original meaning and significance, and help people relate that meaning to the meaning of their lives today. This means that every preacher has the job of building bridges of understanding between the historical meaning of traditional words and the contemporary situation or symbol in which the same meaning is imbedded.

Second, images are another barrier to the meeting of meaning. The images which the participants in communication have of one another or of the subject matter under consideration can effectively obstruct communication. What we say to each other has to filter through what we think the other is like, and therefore what we think the other is saying. Preaching as communication can be blocked by many images: images that the clergy may have of the laity, and the laity may have of the clergy; images both may have of the church, the gospel, religion, or of the relation of the church to the world.

One of the most disabling images with respect to effective preaching is the image which clergy have of laity as passive consumers of preaching rather than as active partners. A common disabling image that lay people frequently hold is that of the preacher as an otherworldly idealist who knows little about life. A crippling common image of the gospel and the Christian religion generally is that its main concern is for the maintenance of middle-class American morality. A prevalent image of the relation of church and world is that the church's business is religion and the preacher ought to stick to it and leave the world and its affairs to practical-minded men. The existence and inhibiting effect of these images are not generally recognized, and therefore preachers and congregations often remain helpless victims of them. All these images and others as well need to be brought out into the open, examined, and dealt with as a part of the preaching curriculum.

A third barrier that blocks the flow of meaning is the differences between people with respect to age, sex, education, cultural level, etc. The difficulty which different generations have in communicating with each other is common knowledge. Male and female are participants in a relationship that is often referred to as the war between the sexes although, as one wit observed, the war has not gone well because of too much fraternization between them. Differences in education create problems of communication. For example, theological education of the clergy can block communication with laity. Cultural differences block the communication between the traditional and the contemporary; or, the church is still emotionally related to the nineteenth-century conditions while the world is involved in the explorations and tensions of the twentieth century. These differences, among others not mentioned, condition the church's preaching.

Again the question for the minister is: What am I

doing, as a part of my preaching responsibility, to work through these barriers?

Fourth, our anxieties are another barrier to the meeting of meaning. These anxieties may be personal, situational, or topical. Our personal anxieties are usually born out of our relationships and our concern about being accepted and loved. Our situational anxieties have to do with the circumstances and security of our lives, how they are to be affected by such technological advances as cybernetics, by inflation, or by war. Our topical anxieties are concerned with subject matter, such as having to talk about difficult or embarrassing problems, or about such loaded subjects as open housing. It is not uncommon for all of these anxieties to beset us at one time. Preaching can easily activate these anxieties in a congregation to the point where the members will not be able to hear what is being said. Therefore, preaching has the responsibility for acknowledging and dealing with them. Unless the preacher breaks the barrier that they offer, the gospel cannot be heard.

Fifth, anxieties can also cause us to be defensive, and this defensiveness, in turn, can both confuse our speaking and block our hearing. All people inevitably develop a system of defenses and defensiveness in order to keep themselves relatively secure. Unfortunately, most people do not seem to be aware of their defensiveness and cannot protect themselves and their relationships against its effect. If we feel under attack, for example, a very natural defense is to reject the criticism by justifying ourselves as we are, with the result that criticism never becomes for us a source of learning. Incidentally, I find that this is a common defense of preachers who apparently are so vulnerable in their preaching that they cannot accept critical comments or even honest discussion that represents another point of view. Congregations, also, can be defensive and engage in self-justification or scape-goating when challenged. It is imperative that preachers and congregations, who together have the responsibility of representing the gospel in the world, should help each other with their defensive reactions to anxiety in order that they may become more open in their communications with one another and with the world and thus more perfect instruments for the diffusion of the Word of God.

These are only five meaning barriers. There are others, such as divergent purposes and preoccupations, all of which make it difficult for us to communicate with each other and require our attention.

Now, the question is: What can we do about them?

7

HOW DIALOGICAL PREACHING
MEETS BARRIERS

Barriers exist in every relationship, and it is tragic that clergymen who have important communication tasks are unaware of them or ignorant of what to do about them because they lack an understanding of the nature and process of communication. The monological communicator is appalled by the existence of barriers, and he will try to drive through them or pretend that they do not exist. The dialogical communicator, on the other hand, knows that they are there, accepts them as a part of the communication situation, and is confident that the barrier, if rightly dealt with, can in the end become a carrier of meaning. We shall now consider how this change is possible.

In a time of theological revolution, when the role of Christ as *secular* rather than "religious" man is being emphasized, when the church is having to abandon the old image of itself as the dictator of the forms of society and to accept for itself a servant role the forms of which society will influence, preaching must rediscover itself as a servant ministry. The preacher can no longer be the Sunday prima donna. His function is a more modest one, and one that depends upon the congregation. In one sense, he is an assistant to a congregation whose voice and message is to be heard in the world in terms that the world can understand.

The preacher's congregation is *in* church; the laymen's "congregation" is *outside* church, *in* the world. Because of this new situation, some in the church are asking today: How can the church organize itself in the secular world so that it does not get in the way of the encounter of God with men? The same kind of question applies to preaching: How is preaching to be understood and ordered so that it not only does not stand in the way of God and man, but promotes the dialogue between them?

The centuries have produced the forms of meeting on Sunday morning for worship, instruction, and preaching. Even if these forms continue to be maintained, they can no longer have the same role in the life of the church as they had in the past. They now require a new context that will effectively supplement the worship, witness, and service of the congregation. But the act of preaching, if it is to contribute to the development of new forms of worship and witness, must itself be open to the possibilities of change, just as an instructor cannot hope to be a teacher unless he himself is open to being a learner.

The preacher ascends his pulpit and begins to speak. Will he speak as a scribe and Pharisee or as one having authority? That is, will he strive to draw people's attention away from the meaning of life and to interest them in a metaphysical or legalistic formulation of religion? Or, will he be the agent who will enable them to evaluate their living, to affirm and correct it, and to recommit themselves to the world as Christians through whom God will make his appeal? These are crucial questions, and how does one answer them?

Here is an illustration drawn from one of our experiences at the Institute. A group of our ministers had attended a nearby church where they listened to a sermon on love as that theme is presented in I Corinthians 13. The preacher quoted Henry Drummond to the effect that love is the greatest power in the world. "There is no situation to which the application of Christian love would not be both relevant and effective," said the preacher, but he gave no illustrations.

After the service a group of laymen met to discuss what meaning the sermon had for them. Immediately, one of the laymen, who was president of a small industry in a highly competitive field, made the comment that the practice of love as commended by the preacher was neither possible nor desirable in the workaday world. When asked why, he described part of the process by which he and his associates secured contracts for new business. He described the planning and scheming, the various competing and conflicting interests, the ulterior motives that operated behind verbal exchanges, the mixture of trust and mistrust, all of which provided, according to him, an unpromising environment for anyone who wanted to practice Christian love.

A number of things became obvious immediately. First, the preacher had not reached this man with his sermon. Second, the man had tested what he thought he heard with a situation to which he was heavily committed as a human being. Third, the preacher had failed to associate what he was saying with this man's point of concern or, in fact, with any other human situation. Fourth, the president of the industrial firm did not recognize that the very situation the preacher was describing as loveless was one that cried aloud for the presence and action of love. In a word, barriers on both sides were operating in all the participants in the business deal. It was interesting to observe that both the clergy and the laity who were participating in this discussion were all too ready to agree with the industrialist that Christian love as delineated in the sermon would not operate in his situation. While such a presentation of the love theme sounds impressive in the pulpit, the participants felt, it does not seem to promise much when rigorously tested in what seemed to be a Godless competitive deal.

At that point in the discussion someone chanced to ask the president how he had managed to survive years of the kind of work and conflict that he had described so vividly. They wanted to know what resources he had had to meet the stresses and strains of his position. One of the ministers put the question this way: "How have you avoided an ulcer or heart attack?" "What is the secret of your survival?"

The man thought a moment and then slowly replied, "I have never been asked this question before." This observation in itself is interesting: it points to the fact that preachers should be interested in the resources that people develop for their living and learn to ask them the kinds of questions that encourage them to identify their resources. "As I think about it now," the man continued, "I would say that I am helped by remembering that my associates, competitors, and customers are persons; that I should respect them and treat them as persons." Although earlier in commenting on the sermon he had said that the practice of Christian love was impractical, he now in his own terms rather than in the theological terms of the preacher was witnessing to the power of personal regard in his business life. Far from disagreeing with the preacher, the industrialist really agreed with him. The difficulty was, however, that he did not recognize what he believed and practiced in the preacher's terms; and the preacher had been unable to provide a secular context for his theological interpretations of love. There had been no dialogue between the preacher and this man. The preacher's sermon lived and died without effect because there was no meeting of meaning between the traditional and the contemporary, between the religious and the secular. The barriers were not worked through.

When the man's response was made known to his minister, the minister's first reaction was one of impatience. He said, "Yes, the man did have some understanding of love, but it was incomplete as compared to the concept of Christian love presented in the sermon." This comment of the minister illustrated a common problem of preachers, namely, that they cannot accept the responses that people make, because of the responses they do *not* make. We tend to throw out what the layman brings to the sermon because of what he does not bring. Instead, the clergy need to learn to accept what people have achieved or may bring, and to affirm and use it in leading them on still further.

It was the discussion after the sermon that showed the industrialist the relation between his own belief and the truth in I Corinthians 13. He was filled with immense excitement. He had been living by his "creed" for a long time without realizing its great significance. Because of the discussion he not only became aware of the significance of what he had said, but he also saw its meaning in relation to the meaning of the gospel theme that he had always considered impractical. The barrier about the impracticality of Christianity was worked through so that a meeting of meaning was accomplished.

In this instance the discussion had to accomplish what the sermon had failed to do. The sermon could have done the same thing if it had taken the live issues of this man's life or some other man's life, and used them dialogically in relation to the passage from Corinthians. Observations the industrialist made about how he practiced respect for persons sounded like the Corinthian passage; and the discussion participants listening to these remarks thought they were listening to a paraphrase of the biblical text. For example, love is "patient"—"You have to give the other guy a chance. I try not to chop him off short." Or, love "is not boastful or arrogant or rude, doesn't insist on its own way, is not irritable or resentful"—"It isn't fair to be braggy. The other guy's usually got something going for himself, and it isn't fair to take it away from him by tooting your own horn so loud that he knows you don't think much of him. Sure, I get angry, but you only make matters worse if you take your feelings out on him. I'd make him angry, and what right have I to do that?"

Although the preacher did not know it, he had an ally for his preaching in his congregation; and how wonderful it would have been had he been able to use the insights of his ally to make clear the truth about Christian love to others.

We now raise the question: How shall the preacher prepare himself for dialogical preaching? The illustration suggests that he should study the theological resources of Scripture, history, and doctrine; and study *also,* with equal seriousness, what he knows of the related meanings from his own authority of both traditional and contemporary experience; and how to recognize the authenticity of the dialogue, both historical and contemporary, between God and man and the dependence of each on the other. His purpose is to bring these dialogues together in order that the historical dialogue may be challenged and judged in the light of the contemporary; and the contemporary dialogue be challenged and given perspective by the historical.

The dialogical preacher knows that to accomplish these tasks he needs the participation of his congregation. The formation and delivery of *his* sermon is not the goal of his preaching. He recognizes that his sermon is only part of a total process. To use a modern analogy, we may think of the preacher's sermon as being like the rocket that starts orbital flight. The purpose of the sermon is to get meaning off the ground and in movement. The minister preaches his sermon in order that other sermons may be brought into being in the congregation, sermons that will be the joint products of both his and the congregation's effort. The following diagram helps to illuminate this.

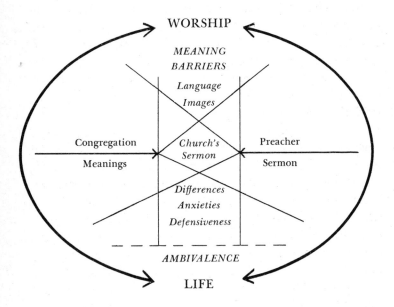

This sermon which is the church's sermon, the joint product of the preacher's message and the congregation's meanings expressed through their listening, is represented in the diagram by the intersection of the two megaphones. We call it the "church's sermon" because it *is* the joint creation of the preacher and members of the congregation. In this concept of preaching the preacher's sermon has a limited purpose and existence. Having put the thought of the congregation into orbit, that is, having activated the thought of the congregation into some form which will inevitably travel with them wherever they go, the minister's sermon, once it is preached, has served its usefulness and is destined for oblivion. It continues to live only insofar as it lives in the fruit of the meeting of meaning between minister and congregation. It is hard for ministers to accept the fact that their sermons as preached never go beyond the church walls, and that the role of the preacher is not exclusively central in the church's preaching. No, the Word must finally live in the lives of people who, when they leave the church, take it with them into the world for which the Word was intended. This will not happen unless the members of the congregation, out of the validity of the meaning of their own experience, are led by the preaching to engage the meaning of the gospel with the meaning of living. In other words, preaching must produce a Word-world dialogue, and it must take place within the people, for it is they who are mainly responsible for taking the Word into the world. The ministry of the ordained is always dependent for implementation on the ministry of the laity. It is becoming increasingly clear with respect to not only the ministry of preaching but all other ministries. The indispensability and centrality of the ministry of laity is indisputable.

But some may be puzzled by this because there will be as many church's sermons as there are persons in the congregation. And others will protest that much of the meeting of meaning may not be as correct—that is, orthodox and complete—as we are accustomed to think it should be. These observations may be true, but that is a part of the risk of communication, and without risk there can be no communication. Perhaps preaching has not had more power because preachers have been afraid to speak and let their message go. Instead, they try to ensure its purity by their precise theological formulations, but these forms of thought may not be appropriate for their people—with the result that the Word is not able to inform the decisions and actions of the laity. But the Word will inform the decisions and actions of the laity if preachers help laymen to think through in their own as well as in traditional terms the meanings of the contemporary dialogue between God and man. This is the task of dialogical preaching.

The diagram also illustrates that the meeting of meaning between preacher and congregation embraces the barriers. Referring to our illustration, we now recognize that part of the process of understanding Christian love from both the traditional and the contemporary points of view includes dealing with some barriers that block understanding. In this instance there were the barriers of language, including the phrase "Christian love." There were the image barriers having to do with ministers, church, Bible, from the layman's side; and with images of laymen, of nonreligious, of preacher, from the preacher's side. There were the barriers of anxiety and defensiveness on the part of both. Most of these in this case were worked through casually without particular design and method, and mostly by the layman because the preacher seemed defensive and never did directly engage him.

The main point of this chapter is that preaching that engages people's meanings dialogically will be able to deal with the resistances caused by ambivalence and all the barriers that occur in communication. Sometimes this kind of preaching has to deal directly and consciously with the barriers; sometimes it overcomes them incidentally.

8

PREACHING AND
LISTENING DIALOGICALLY

At this stage in our developing thought it will, perhaps, be helpful to underscore certain of our insights into preaching and listening dialogically.

Early in the discussion with the industrialist he was asked what resource enabled him to endure the strenuousness of his life without destructive effects. He responded that this was the first time such a question had been asked him. The raising of such a searching question should be one of the purposes of preaching. Men should be asked by what principles they live; who are their gods. They should be given opportunity and assistance to formulate their convictions, to make their own interpretations of their experience, in order that its meaning may be the basis of further learning and growth. That, it will be recalled, was the method commonly used by our Lord. He asked men questions that gave them opportunity to formulate their meanings: Of the smart young lawyer: "Who was neighbor to him that fell among the thieves?" Of the disciples: "Who do you say that I am?" Or, "Where shall we buy bread that these shall eat?" I believe that one of the first responsibilities of the Christian teacher is to help men raise the theological question on the basis of which they may hope to understand the relevance of the gospel. A well-asked question can often do more than lengthy advice. And question-raising is a ministry in which the laity can participate, too.

The Principle of Inclusion

A second insight to be underscored is that dialogical preaching requires the employment of the principle of inclusion. I am indebted to Martin Buber for my understanding of this principle. It means that when we address another we do so in ways that include their meanings.* A part of our preparation for speaking should be to find out what people bring to us in the way of questions, hypotheses, affirmations, and doubts; and our communication, whether formal like a sermon or informal like a conversation, should include these as part of its content. The preacher's sermon in our illustration gave no evidence that he knew anything about or understood contemporary human life. He did not draw on the recognizable experiences of his people in order to provide a context for his explication of a traditional doctrine, that is, he did not preach *inclusively*. He preached *exclusively*. Had he, through accident or design, known of the industrialist's faith and practice, he could have used it to promote dialogue between the doctrine and the man's experience, and through these have also reached other men. Use of the man's faith and practice could have served two purposes: It could have provided an illustration of what

See diagram, p. 72. Inclusion is represented by the intersecting lines from each side.

was meant by love; and the preacher could have used the Scripture to affirm and illumine the faith of a man in whose experience was evidence of God's presence. For an important purpose of preaching is to identify the presence and activity of God in secular life.

Preaching that employs inclusion also has the ability to lay open the meaning of the contemporary so that it can recognize and respond to the larger, timeless meanings that often come to us out of the tradition and even be completed by them. To return to our illustration, the industrialist was excited when he discovered that his insight about keeping people in focus as persons was a part of the Christian way of life. Thus the partial meanings that emerge out of our own experience can be joined to the larger meanings that have been accumulating through the centuries as a result of each generation's participation in the dialogue between God and man.

Contemporary meanings have for both the preacher and his listeners more importance today than ever before because man's contemporary search for meaning confronts so much new data that has never been properly related to the traditional sources of meaning. The preacher, therefore, faces a different kind of congregation from one he would have fifty years ago, but because of the situation we are discussing, he has one of history's greatest opportunities to preach the gospel. He must learn to look for the values in what people value, and help them to affirm their truth, power, and need so that with it they may move into greater truth.

Preaching as a Cooperative Activity

A third insight to be noted is that preaching is a cooperative activity on the part of congregation and preacher. The dialogical preacher knows that he cannot preach the gospel by himself. Some preachers have learned this lesson. They would not think of preaching without first having drawn on some congregational assistance. It could be through a group's study of a passage of Scripture from which the text was to be selected. The relevance of the passage to the lives of the people would become apparent in the course of the group discussion: the questions that it raised, the insights that it activated, the blocks to understanding that existed would all become known to the preacher who would stand in the pulpit and speak not so much *to* the people but *for* the people of God whose thought and experience constituted a part of the authenticity of the sermon.

For example, when a murderer is executed and the question of capital punishment is raised, about which there is such divided opinion, the preacher should bring the meanings of the gospel and the meanings of the issue together in order that members of the congregation will think more about it and be better able to express their views with conviction and effect. The preacher thus speaks not to, but for and with the community of God.

The occasion for a sermon may come also from a chance remark. A minister was visiting a parishioner who was a sculptress and who was doing a figure of a mother and child. The work was at the stage where the figure of the child, looking up into the mother's face, was beginning to emerge clearly from the surrounding stone. It was an exciting time. The sculptress, in the ecstasy of the moment, exclaimed, "I am so happy, it's sinful!" As she proceeded with her work the minister asked her why she had referred to her happiness as sinful.

"I don't know," she replied, "except that I have always felt guilty about being as happy as I am. So many people seem unhappy with their lives bogged down in pain and sorrow. But as an artist I see and hear so much that delights me that my response to life is ecstatic." She was able to say this in spite of conditions in her life that could have discouraged her.

"I have run into this guilty reaction to joy before," commented the minister. "Implicit in it is a grim concept of God."

"Lots of people feel this way," added the sculptress. "I have friends who love their children so much that they are afraid God will take them away. If God is love, why should we feel guilty when we love so much or are happy? . . . Why don't you preach about this? It would help me, and many others, too."

The minister agreed, but asked if he might describe at the beginning of his sermon the situation out of which the question arose.

Several weeks later he preached on the concepts of God that are implicit in people's characteristic attitudes and behaviors, and showed how primitive these concepts are when compared with the concepts they profess of a merciful and loving God. He went on to provide some suggestions as to how his hearers might move from primitive to more Christian relationships with God and their fellows.

The response to the sermon was spectacular. The congregation's attention was rapt. Meanings in them were being searched out, examined, formulated, and joined to new and releasing meanings. Fears that had imprisoned people for years were being unlocked. The boundaries of thought were being extended and courage was being stretched so that people began to sense a dimension in living that was new. Different members of the congregation mentioned briefly something of the relevance the sermon had for them, and several made appointments for counseling. One man in particular told of living for years with the conviction that his only son had been killed in an automobile accident because he had loved him too much.

The point of the story is that the preacher's sermon and the church's sermons (the messages born in each of the hearers) resulted from the minister's having heard and responded to the theological question implicit in the sculptress's remark, "I am so happy, it's sinful."

Preaching for the People

Another illustration of speaking to the congregation *for* people comes from an experience in preparing a young couple for marriage. Their discussions together, with the aid of the minister, had meant a great deal to them; in particular they came to a vivid realization of the power of personal relations for their individual weal or woe. One of them had been the product of destructive family relationships, the effect of which threatened the well-being of the new marriage. The other had enjoyed good family relations. Between them they saw the positive and negative influence they could have on each other and their

children. They resolved, too, that their relations were to
be a means of grace to each other. Toward the close of
the sessions, they expressed appreciation for the exciting
new insights that had come to them, and also expressed
the wish that they might tell other people about them.
The minister asked the couple to put into their own
words the thoughts they would like to share. When they
had finished he explained that he could share their
thoughts for them by preaching a sermon in which they
would be embodied. He obtained their permission to tell
the congregation the source of the sermon without reveal-
ing their names.

They were present on the Sunday morning that the
minister preached the sermon on "Personal Relations—
A Means of Grace." He began by announcing to the congregation that he was preaching this sermon for a young
couple who wanted to share with them some exciting new
understandings that had come to them while they were
preparing for marriage. He then proceeded to preach the
sermon, developing their thoughts in relation to common
needs that he knew existed among the members of the
congregation. The congregation was breathlessly attentive,
and responses afterward indicated that they heard a message that carried extra authority because it came out of
the life of the community and it was the word to the community. More of this kind of preaching is possible and
would be appreciated.

Or, the minister might discuss a doctrine in contemporary terms with some laymen—for example, of grace in
relation to works; or, he might check with them a theme
that he planned to present and some of the crucial words
that he would use in order to test for the understandings
that will and will not be present in the congregation. One
man I know makes it a regular practice to test with se-

lected members of his congregation the meanings they
have for certain words he is going to use in his preaching.
Later, in his sermon, these meanings are identified, affirmed, or corrected and completed, and his congregation
always knows that he is speaking inclusively with them.
They become participants with him in the dialogue between the word of man and the Word of God. Sometimes
an issue in the life of the community dictates the subject
of the sermon, and the meaning of the people's experience in relation to the issue becomes a part of the source
of the preacher's preparation. Again, he speaks not to,
but for and with, the community of God.

The theological implication here is important, if we
believe that God may speak to the world through the
church, and to the church through the world. People who
come to church are a part of the world, and sometimes
more a part of the world than they are of the church.
They are often unknowingly, as well as knowingly, the
agents of God's action in the world. There is no con-
ceivable way by which the Word of God through the
world can influence the church unless the preacher and
other ministers are open and attentive to the word that
may be spoken to them out of the contemporary context
of the world.

It is my belief that we have been identifying our Lord's
own kind of preaching. He made no point of being "religious." He stood in the midst of life. He looked for the
meanings of men. He employed their symbols. He helped
men to identify their meanings and then demonstrated
how their meanings pointed to ultimate meaning. And
that is the task that we have received from his hand.

9

IMPLICATIONS OF DIALOGUE FOR PREACHER AND LISTENER

This concept of preaching immediately raises questions about practice: How is the church to replace stereotypes of preaching with the dialogical practice that will free the Word from religious imprisonment for its work in the world into which it was born in the first place?

The Preacher's Role

It is the preacher's responsibility, as we have seen, to study the Scriptures, the teaching and experience of the church, in order that he may speak out of them the Word of God to his own day. We have said that if he is to be a dialogical preacher it is necessary that he make himself familiar with the meanings that his people will bring to the homiletical encounter out of their experiences. This means that he must become responsive to what they bring, and devise ways in which he can hear and use the laity's potential contribution.

Furthermore, the preacher must be responsive to the

needs and contributions of *all* his people. He must be attentive not only to women and children, but to men; and not only to the sick and needy, but to the strong and influential. Too large a share of the ministry of the ordained clergy has been confined to those who are more readily dependent upon it. Many ministers admit that they are intimidated by people who do not show an obvious need for their services. Ministers also have to learn to relate to people who think they are unnecessary and have nothing to say that is relevant to the contemporary situation. The preacher must combine in himself both confidence in the Word and anxiety that it might not be heard. And he should learn to do this not only to defend the Christian position, but to understand and stand with his people as they take their place in the world, even though standing with them will sometimes have to be out of his weakness and lack of answers for the profound questions they are raising. He must learn to preach out of the weakness of his understanding of the gospel and of life as well as out of his strengths. Then people who are not predisposed toward him may find him to be more authentic. Many people find the pretensions, assumed power, and answers of preachers laughable. They might take the preacher more seriously if he would be honest about what he has to offer, namely, that sometimes he has little to offer, and can only stand humbly before the human question with the hope that God will be able to speak and act out of his honest weakness.

The clergyman's preparation should also be concerned with the study of the secular publications. Too much of the reading of clergy is religious and theological. There is need not only to read theology for theology's sake, but to read other things theologically, such as newspapers, magazines, journals; to look for the correlatable meanings of movies, plays, television, and radio programs. It is important for the preacher to be informed about the things that most of his people are doing, seeing, and thinking outside of church. He should try to find out from his people what their activities or reactions mean to them, whether it be a television program or a state fair or an international crisis or an episode of racial tension. How appalling it is that significant events in the life of the world are ignored in the worship and preaching of the church. Only preparation that is based on both traditional and contemporary meaning will produce a sermon that will be an adequate instrument to activate the dialogue between man and God.

In considering the preacher's delivery of his sermon, we must remember that the purpose of his sermon is to activate a partnership with the hearer that will produce the church's sermon which, in turn, will become an orbiting message in the world. If the preacher believes that he is preaching *with* his people, he is more apt to address them directly. In direct address one looks at people and is guided by their response. Verbal response from the congregation is not possible or desirable during the sermon, even though there have been some experiments in overt dialogue between preacher and congregation. In my opinion these have occasional value but are not likely to become normative.

Anyone who is at all observant, however, is aware of how much people respond nonverbally, especially if they are interiorly free to do so. There are always certain people in the congregation upon whom a preacher depends because, in various nonverbal ways, they indicate that they are hearing and responding to him. So real is their help that when they are not present he misses them. When he tells these people how much the quality of their attention and response assists him, they are often surprised that he has been aware of or assisted by them. The imperceptible nod or shake of the head, the smile, the puckered brow, the stillness of concentration, the restlessness of inattention are all meaningful statements about their participation in the act of preaching. A congregation can be trained to improve its communicative responsiveness and provide their preacher unusual assistance. My experience reveals that when people are made aware of their potential powers of communication in even the "audience" role, communication occurs both more readily and more profoundly. Congregations can be helped to realize that they have a responsibility to help the preacher preach his sermon. The story is told of a church in Philadelphia which at one time had a succession of great preachers and found itself with an incumbent who, after one year, had not measured up to the quality of preaching that the congregation expected. When a committee consulted with him, and he learned their evaluation, he offered to resign. The story goes that the committee—and what a wise one it was—refused to accept his resignation and told him that it was up to them to help him become the preacher they believed he could be. Embodied in that story is the true doctrine of the ministry. It is tragic that more ministers do not recognize their creative dependence upon their congregations and find ways to evoke that assistance.

A preacher must also be prepared to use whatever response he may elicit. Although I have already suggested that verbal response from the congregation is not usual in most preaching occasions, it does occur; and perhaps a form of preaching may develop in which it would be more expected. When it does occur the preacher needs both courage and perspective in order to be creatively responsive. For example, during a sermon on race relations which was being preached to a large congregation, a man rose to his feet to dispute a point being made by the preacher. The preacher was startled and the congregation was stunned. Quickly, however, the preacher recovered and spoke to the man's question and an exchange of opinions took place between them. After several moments the preacher asked the man to listen to the rest of the sermon and then they could resume their discussion after the service. When the sermon ended the congregation spontaneously rose to its feet and applauded in praise of the preacher's acceptance of the unexpected response as a normal part of the preaching situation.

We have here an example of a speaker's ability to transform what could have been a barrier into a carrier of communication. He demonstrated in action as well as in words the truths of relationship of which he was speaking. There was a meeting of meaning between him and the people who were listening to him; and there was born in them then a lesson that they will never forget. The preacher who sees communication as a partnership business will be resourceful in the use of whatever happens in the communication relationship.

If there were more dialogical partnership in the act of preaching, preachers would become less dependent upon their manuscripts. I do not wish this statement to be interpreted to mean that there would be less need for preparation. The kind of preaching we are thinking about calls for even greater preparation because dependence would be upon the relationship rather than upon a manuscript.

The Role of the Laity

First, the laymen's preparation is usually thought of in terms of praying for the preacher that he may speak the truth, and praying for themselves that they may be receptive to the message. Occasionally one hears about laymen being asked to study in advance the Scripture from which the text of the sermon is to be taken. All of these activities are helpful. But we also ought to include as part of the laity's preparation for the preaching some consideration of the kind of lives they lead between Sundays. This preparation centers on their examining their involvement in the life of the world and their commitment to its affairs, for out of such examination they will make their contribution to the dialogue. There are many church people who are so church-oriented that they do not recognize the religious significance of their secular responsibilities. The laity's participation in the church's preaching will depend both upon the meanings they find in their lives and upon their ability to live in the world reflectively.

People who live reflectively are people who search for and find meaning in their experience. For example, a person blind to the contradictions between what he professes and what he does can be insufferably self-righteous. Another person can be aware of such contradictions and realize that his actions are not in harmony with his profession; this person can acknowledge and confess his guilt and accept forgiveness when caught in circumstances beyond his control. The first man might not be able to hear the gospel because of his self-righteousness; the second man's meanings may open his ears so that he begins to understand the gospel in real depth. The first man, because he is unreflective and closed to the meanings of his life, will not hear the preacher. The second man, because of his insight, will be able to hear and respond. Our studies at the Institute have revealed that the more meaning people can bring to the preaching, the more they will hear; and the more they hear the better will they be able to live reflectively. For these people the cumulative effect of the church's preaching is the fruit of dialogue. The gospel assists them in their living, and their living assists them in their understanding of and response to the gospel.

The laymen's preparation for the church's preaching is also dependent upon their use of other resources. All men are looking for meaning, and some do so more effectively than others. The reflective reading of the newspaper and other secular literature, the reading of various kinds of interpretive literature that helps one sort out his values and the meanings of his life—all constitute a part of the laymen's preparation for hearing the Word and for witnessing to it in his world.

The church's preaching requires this kind of reflection and study on the part of the laity, and it cannot be done for them by the minister. At times of installation or ordination of a pastor members of the congregation should be charged about their responsibilities as seriously as the minister is about his, and they should be made to realize that his ministry is dependent upon theirs. The ministry of the ordained, to be effective, requires the ministry of the lay members.

Finally, the laity have a responsibility for the delivery of the preacher's sermon. Earlier I spoke of this matter from the point of view of the preacher's dependence upon the laity's response; now I write for the laity to urge them

to practice active listening. In a sense it is true that laity
have a responsibility to pull the preaching out of the
minister by the urgency of their questions, by their sense
of excitement resulting from their experience of the meeting of meaning in their lives, by their devotion to their
work in the world, and by their regular participation in
the worship-preaching dialogue. What is not always realized is that the quality of the hearing has a great deal to
do with the quality of the speaking, and that this is a
ministry of the laity. It is just as true that a hearer can
project himself in his hearing as a speaker can project
himself in his speaking. If the preaching of the gospel is
urgent, so also is the hearing of the gospel, and an urgent
hearer can make an urgent speaker. Each needs the other.
Imagine what it would be like for a preacher to meet a
congregation Sunday after Sunday that had been trained
to be his assistants in the preaching of the gospel.

The concept of preaching ministry that we are building
here is being practiced in a growing number of places.
In one local church where dialogical preaching has become
the norm, a layman said to his preacher after the service,
"We didn't do so well today." "What do you mean?"
asked the preacher. "I mean," replied the parishioner,
"your sermon was not as helpful as it might have been
because I wasn't working along with you. In fact, I think
I was pushing down in me the meaning of something that
happened to me this past week." This parishioner was
right! Preaching is a cooperative business requiring the
joint thought and action of preacher and people.

10

HOW TO START
DIALOGICAL PREACHING

It is always difficult to change people's concepts and behavior, which is no less true when it comes to changing people's expectations and behavior in relation to preaching. Many ministers acknowledge that the pull of the stereotype is so great, despite their best efforts to escape it, that they are drawn helplessly into its vortex. This being true, for laity as well as clergy, we need to find ways of effecting change and the structures needed for dialogical preaching. In this chapter we shall discuss these methods and structures.

Instructing the Laity on Their Role

First, it is imperative that the ministry of preaching be discussed with the laity. For many years I have checked with both clergy and laity about the instruction given and received on the ministry of preaching. Rarely have I found a layman who has ever been instructed on how to listen to a sermon. Apparently it is assumed that because he has ears he can hear, and that while there is a technique to the delivery of a sermon, there is nothing that the layman has to learn about listening to it. Likewise, I have seldom found a minister who has instructed his people as to their part in the church's preaching. Again, it is assumed by the clergy that the role of the laity in preaching is so simple that it requires no instruction. I have examined a great many church-membership courses, and the matter of the preaching from the layman's point of view is not even mentioned, let alone discussed. I suggest, therefore, that we begin to train the laity for their part in the church's preaching.

A first step would be to take sermon time to talk with the congregation about the ministry of preaching, describing both the minister's and the layman's role, and the relationship of the two. As a teacher, for example, I learned that it was desirable to take time out from teaching to consider with the students the process of teaching and learning. I found that they needed to reconsider our objectives, my role as teacher, their role as students, the complementary relation of our two roles, and to learn from the meaning of some of the events of our relationship. Such occasional discussions greatly facilitated the educational process. We need to have the same concern for process in the preaching relationship. One might even take a blackboard into the sanctuary in order to assist by diagram* their thinking through of the mutual relationships and responsibilities involved in preaching, using the insights of this book.† For a congregation that has much to learn in this matter it might be necessary to provide such sessions two or three times a year until understanding of the process begins to bear fruit.

* For example, the diagram on p. 58.
† There is no reason why a projector could not be used if a blackboard would be too small to be seen.

Classes for new members provide another opportunity to instruct and train persons for participation in preaching. New members need to understand the purpose of preaching, what the preacher's role is, how they may prepare for and assist in the delivery of the gospel to the world in terms of the secular. The education of the laity for their part in the ministry of the church, including the ministry of preaching, is every bit as important as the education of the clergy, for without a trained laity, skillfully obedient to their ministry in the world, the ministry of the clergy is vain indeed.

The Role of Study Groups

A second way to recover dialogue in preaching is through the use of study groups. One of the characteristics of church renewal is the variety of study and discussion groups in which laymen now participate. Much of this study and discussion is concerned with the areas of life that are properly the object of the church's mission. Instead of preoccupation with religion or the church for its own sake, many of these programs are increasingly concerned with conditions of human life; Christian vocation through occupational concerns; the meaning of existence; the nature of man; the resolution of conflicts; the tensions between the individual and the corporate; the personal and the technical; the power of the personal in relation to the powers of mechanization. All of this dedicated concern has a tremendous potential for the renewal of the church and for dialogue in preaching if preacher and people will see it as a mutual project. Too many clergy, however, quietly absent themselves from these discussions and fail to partake of the fruit of them; or, if present, take over the discussions. Clergy are heard to say that they are glad they do not have to endure the elementary and primitive responses of lay people as they struggle through the meanings of the gospel in relation to their lives; that the thoughts of the laity, as they cope with the meaning of the gospel, are boring. Some even say that this provision for discussion is done for the sake of the laity who seem to want it, but they do not expect very much good to come of it because "zero and zero can never add up to anything." Such attitudes and comments are appallingly unperceptive. Anyone who calls another human being's sincere search for truth stupid is himself stupid and unworthy of the trust of preacher and teacher.

The findings and conclusions of these study groups are indispensable for the preacher. For example, no one can really preach "justification by grace through faith" who has not engaged with laymen in the process by which laymen move in their discussion from dependence on the law for their justification, work through their first impressions of grace as foolishness, and come finally to a new freedom because of it. Yet many clergy cannot endure the rambling discussions, the misinterpretations, the confusions that inevitably attend any honest wrestling with theological truth. They suffer from acute "agenda anxiety," fearing that both the truth and the form in which they hold it will be lost. But participation with laymen in such theological struggles is an exercise that the preacher may not avoid. An indispensable part of his preparation for his task as preacher is to work through with lay people an existential understanding of the faith they profess. I would recommend that every preacher who means business provide himself with at least four to six weeks of this kind of encounter with laymen each year. Such an experience makes a preacher humble, perceptive, and responsive; and such a preacher creates an attentive and witnessing congregation.

The Importance of Feedback

Third, recovery of dialogue in preaching may be achieved through provision for feedback on the preaching. The preacher may invite a group of at least six people to meet after church and react to the service and the sermon in order that he may have a response from the congregation to his communication. The easiest way to make this feedback available to the preacher is to provide the discussion group with a tape recorder that will record its discussion to which he can listen sometime later. Some clergy have tried to get this feedback by meeting with the discussants personally. Our experience indicates that no matter how mature a relationship a preacher has, his presence inevitably inhibits the group's discussion of their response to his message. On the other hand, people quickly get used to a tape recorder, especially if only the microphone is visible, so that discussion is not blocked. It is not necessary for the group to have a leader, as is commonly thought by overanxious ministers. We find that the most effective leadership is the leadership of some well-thought-out questions. The group need have only a moderator, a responsibility which a member may assume.

Examples of questions that the preacher may give such a group are:

What did the preacher say to *you?* (Do not try to reproduce what the preacher said; this question asks for what *you* heard.)

What difference do you think the sermon will make in your life, or was it of only passing and theoretical interest?

In what ways were you challenged or drawn to greater devotion to your areas of responsibility?

Did his style and method, language, manner of delivery, and illustrations help or hinder the hearing of his message? Explain.

Do you think the preacher received any assistance from the congregation in the preparation and delivery of his sermon? If so, describe; if not, why not?

And, finally, ask the members of the group to communicate through the tape anything that over the years they have wanted to tell the clergy about their communication.

These or any other questions carefully formulated are the best means I know of to evoke an honest discussion. Usually, much more is discussed than what the questions ask for. Forty-five minutes allows ample time for productive discussion.

I cannot emphasize too much that the best discussions by laymen and, therefore, the best feedback, come from groups that meet without the preacher being present. If he is there, the discussion will be inhibited no matter how good a relationship he may have with the participants. Furthermore, members of the group will tend to address themselves to him, and that easily results in a question-and-answer type of discussion. When the preacher is not present the people will discuss the sermon with each other, thus giving him a more honest recording of how laymen think and respond not only to him but to one another.

A group of six or eight people seems to be most satisfactory for this purpose. They should be invited during the preceding week in order that they may make baby-sitting and other arrangements. The discussion should take place immediately after the service in order to save the time of the participants. Effort should be made to select a cross section of people from the congregation; people who are outside the church may also participate, as well as individuals who are alienated from the church, provided they can be persuaded to come and listen to a sermon for this purpose. Young people make excellent discussants because of their frankness. Preachers should find out how effective their communication is with young people and accept the help of young listeners to increase their effectiveness. Before initiating this kind of feedback, it is advisable, as well as desirable, to inform the whole congregation that the group (or groups) have been invited to discuss the sermon. Incidentally, a minister who offers himself for honest dialogue with his congregation increases their respect and inspires their trust.

When such discussions on a sermon take place, it is imperative that the preacher listen to these discussions and let his congregation know through his subsequent preaching that he has heard them. The feedback will often indicate to him what he needs to do in the way of correcting and completing his people's understandings. He will also discover what are the crucial issues his people face, and he will receive countless leads to areas of interest and need that he might otherwise never learn about. Such discussions regularly held not only help the preacher know the response to sermons he has preached, but also serve to guide him in preparing future sermons. In a word, the feedback process can begin to change the quality of a congregation's listening which, in turn, inevitably changes the quality of preaching.* We have found also that as people are helped to discuss what they hear, they hear more; and the more they hear, the more they take with them into their living; and the more reflectively they live, the more they hear the Word that is preached; and, therefore, the more assistance does the preacher have from his people in the preaching of the Word.

* Clyde Reid, in his study "Two-way Communication through Small Groups in Relation to Preaching," confirms the Institute's use of small feedback groups. He states that participation in group discussion of sermons increased the participants' understanding of sermons, and feels that the sermon "spoke to their condition more, and increased interest and attention during preaching."

11

THE CHURCH'S SERMON
TO THE WORLD

If there is a uniqueness about preaching and the sermon, it lies in the fact that both are the means of a unique action—the action of God through the structures of human relationships. Understanding this, we can now define the nature of the church's sermon to the world.

The act of preaching is itself an act of the gospel. Preaching is not only a declaration about the action of God in Christ, but its very delivery is action and is a part of God's action. Speaking can be merely verbal. I can say, "I love you," but because I am only saying words, you are not grasped by the meaning of my statement, "I love you." But I can say, "I love you," in a way and with a meaning that make the saying of the words an act of love, and the hearing of them an experience of being loved. Preaching the gospel is meant to be the latter kind of communication. We dare to say these things about preaching—we can say them about every ministry and about the church itself—not because of any power we have, but because of the way God has chosen to work with men. His Spirit draws us together in a unique fellowship, and acts in, through, and between us as persons. God makes his

53955

appeal through us. Preaching, therefore, is a way of sharing the personal action of God who insists on a living,
personal encounter with us in a sphere of temporal personal relationships. The Spirit today continues through
us the releasing action which was begun in Jesus Christ
in the sphere of personal relationship. Preaching should
mean the contemporary appearance of Christ's spirit in
human relationships with all that he offers of understanding, confrontation, judgment, forgiveness, encouragement, and transformation.

God does not act through the preacher alone, but
through the hearers as well. The whole act of preaching,
therefore, must include both what the preacher does and
what the hearers do. Without the action of either side
there is no preaching, and no living sermon will come
into being.

The Preacher

The action of the preacher is rooted in the whole context of his life with man and God. The composition of
his sermon for any occasion is a momentary focus of some
part of the meaning of his relationships. It is imperative,
though, that the preacher's sermon be more than a composition—a thing—which he gives to his congregation.
His sermon is his created form for an encounter with the
laity, a meeting of persons with an identifiable purpose
and message. It is not enough that he should be the com-
poser of the form of the message, standing outside of it.
Instead, his chosen word must become his committed action. His word must become flesh that meets the embodied
word of his hearers. Both clergy and laity must learn to
live up to the daring concept: *I am the message.*

So, likewise, the action of the laymen as listening participants in preaching is rooted in the context of their lives with God and man. They bring their meanings—their questions, answers, problems, insights—to the hearing of the preacher's sermon. Then they must strive to identify the meeting of meaning between themselves and the preacher, and organize it for retention as new resource for living. And, finally, theirs is responsibility for delivering, verbally and nonverbally, to the world whatever living word was born in them. And they, too, must dare to believe and act: *I am the message.*

Preaching, therefore, is the process by which preacher and people together bring into being the church's sermon as distinct from the preacher's sermon. Each person who responds to this preaching encounter will bear in himself some part of the church's sermon which he is to share with someone either through spoken word or through action. Only in this way can we carry the sermon beyond the walls of the church because the kind of preaching being discussed here will be done both in and out of the church.

The preacher must be relieved of the full burden of the sermon, and train himself to train the laity to assume their indispensable role in this ministry so that on every preaching occasion there will be a living encounter between the word of man and the Word of God. We need to declericalize preaching. Laymen cannot be allowed to stand on the sidelines and irresponsibly either criticize or praise the preacher. They must be encouraged and trained for constructive participation.

Furthermore, the preacher should not allow himself to be defensive and continue in the lonely, isolated role that a mistaken tradition has forced upon him. What is required is a partnership in preaching in which the minister's part is seen to be as dependent upon the laity as the laity are on the preacher's.

And, finally, as has been said before, we are being called to take part in a life with God and man in which we, both clergy and laity, dare to say with our Lord: *I am the message.* Of course, the message is more than we are or have, but in a very real sense we are the message or there is no message for those who would listen to us.

The Laity

We come now in our discussion to the laymen's responsibility for delivering the church's sermon in the world. More experimentation and exploration of what it means for the laity to preach the church's sermon through word and action needs to be initiated. And we need also to learn how to train laymen to respond to the church's teaching through conscious decision and action. We can no longer afford to leave this part of the church's ministry to chance.

Delivery by word. The word is meant to be representative of the person and his meanings. Men talk about what they really believe in, and one knows it by the linguistic urgency with which they speak. But men may not talk about what they merely profess to believe in. In discussions with laymen I have learned from them that they often do not talk about their religious professions because they do not really believe them. They say of themselves that if they really believe in something, they find the words with which to express it. The industrialist in our earlier illustration is able to communicate his conviction about the importance of being person-centered. He does not do it with religious language, but his meaning is conveyed nonetheless. We should listen for the ring of conviction in men's voices and then pay attention to the area of life about which they are speaking. This will give us a clue. Dialogue produces convictions, and convictions are expressed in dialogue.

The answer to the question as to how laymen may be encouraged to witness in the world as Christians is that they must be involved in an engagement that produces in them convictions that inevitably have to be expressed. Monological preaching and teaching of the church does not produce this kind of lay witness because it does not pick up their interests, employ their insights, and involve them in its formulations. But these same men are interested in something. They do have insights, they are involved in issues, and they do witness to their beliefs. The industrialist believed in the work of reconciliation, in the importance of persons, and he understood his own and other men's crucial roles in the formation and operation of the structures of industry. And through the dialogue of his meanings with those of the gospel's, the value of what he had always believed in became even more meaningful when he discovered its relation to the gospel. That understanding intensified his conviction and increased his enthusiasm. He now tells the story of what he saw and heard, and men's hearts and minds are quickened by the fervency of his witness. He has not acquired a new vocabulary. He does not use the terms of theology. He does have a new awareness of the meaning of what he has always believed in, and he now has a context for it. He now knows that he is a part of a great fellowship of kindred believers, and he no longer feels as alone in his witness. It seems to me that we have in this illustration an indi-

cation of what a preacher's task is, namely, to help men
to be aware of the causes to which they give their lives,
which are often also the causes of God; to affirm and
quicken their enthusiasm; to free them for further discoveries of meaning.

Dialogical preaching can produce a "going" church: a
church whose members go into all the human enterprises
such as business and industry, science, art, education, poli-
tics and government, and engage in these with a sense of
both their immediate and their ultimate purpose. In the
heart of those affairs they talk the talk that is needed to
accomplish their business. That is the immediate purpose.
But there is a deeper purpose, a purpose that is linked to
the purpose of God and his kingdom. The Christian is
not always expected to engage in God-talk. Instead, he
talks about life and business and art as if these areas are
God's domain, too, for there is a way of living and working in them that brings men together because they see the
presence of God in daily life and they find a new dimension for work and life.

Again we Christians have important questions to study
and answer that are raised by our technological knowledge
and skill. The creation of life and possibly human life is
imminent. Prenatal genetic control may perhaps be able
to arrange the sex, skills, and personality of those to be
born. Character change by medical means is coming. The
indefinite prolongation of life is now a real possibility. If
the church is to deal with these questions adequately, dialogue rather than monologue is needed. The man-questions are tremendous, and our present grasp of the God-
answer is not equal to it. Monological theology is too
small and frail to cope with the great man-questions; but
dialogical preaching will help people to think theologi-

cally about the human questions and to make decisions that will guide their acting out the gospel in the human arenas.

A conference of schoolteachers on "Christianity and Education" became impatient because the discussion was directed to their responsibility for students through their relationship to them and their directing of the learning process. They wanted, they said, to talk of "Christianity and Education." It is easier to "talk about" Christianity than it is to practice it. It was easier for these teachers to have an academic discussion "about" Christianity and the purposes of education than it was for them to face what the gospel requires of them as teachers in the concreteness of their responsibility for students. Unless their Christian beliefs inform and direct their attitudes and work as teachers, their Christianity is worthless.

Delivery by action. We come naturally now to consider the laymen's delivery of the church's sermon to the world through action. That action consists mostly of their decisions and actions in the enterprises of everyday living. The language of action will be both conscious and unconscious. What a man is will manifest itself in the way in which he meets the daily issues of life. If the moments of worship and preaching produce a real meeting between the meaning of man's life and the Word and Sacrament of God for him, we can rest assured that this will manifest itself in his life. He can never be as if this meeting of meaning had not occurred. We may not be able to identify the results but we may be sure that they are there.

Sometimes in discussions with laymen we hear of incidents which indicate how true this is. A man told me recently of a change in attitude that was expressed by him during a meeting of his organization about policy in relation to their marketing practice. He became aware that he was speaking for more consideration of persons and less for profits. The change in him was so great that it was noticed and commented on by others. He, too, was surprised by the shift in his point of view. Afterward he was able to trace it back to a moment of insight that came to him during a service following a heated discussion in a study group two weeks earlier. We can be sure that this kind of thing happens all the time, even though we do not know about it. The opportunity, however, for members of a congregation to wrestle, out of their own meanings and in their own terms, with the meanings of the gospel must be provided. For out of such wrestling emerges committed action.

Preaching through action is also an act of will and decision. We may choose to do something as a deliberate representation of a truth that has been born in us. I remember talking with a layman one time who said that he had never been able to understand our Lord's command that we should love our enemies. Then, when in a sermon he learned that love is more than affectionate feelings, that it can also be expressed by assuming one's responsibility for an enemy, he saw the truth behind the commandment. He had an enemy whom he hated with all his heart, but he saw that there was something he could and should do for the man, even though he did not feel like doing it. He discovered to his amazement that not only could he do it, but that when he had done it his relationship with his enemy began to change. Here he was preaching the church's sermon through an action that he had willed to do.

But the action we are thinking about is more than individual; it must be social. We live in a time when men must act together in the use of power for the accomplishment of justice and peace. The local church congregation as a group is not strong, and may be physically isolated from the areas of need. So the church member must find his place in as many power structures as possible through which he can act out the gospel by participation in the lively issues of human affairs. Monological preaching cultivates attitudes of isolationism and indifference. Dialogical preaching challenges, disturbs, and provokes men to decision. If they say No to the gospel then at least they are honest and the church is rid of "dead wood." Anyone who knows anything at all about grass-roots church membership cannot help realizing how much the church is bogged down with the enormous weight of narrow-minded, petty, provincial, selfish people who want a church devoted to status quo unrelatedness. If through dialogical preaching some people say Yes to the gospel, they will take their places in the diverse social structures of towns and cities. With Christ they will be present in the life of the world. Through them God will make his appeal.

In Summary

The world and not the church is the object of the church's mission. It is also clear that the proper relationship between the church and the world is one of dialogue; that this dialogue occurs partly through the flow of people to and fro between the church when it gathers and the church as it is dispersed in the world where church people find their true ministry in their life involvements. The meaning contained in this flow is the concern of the church's preaching. With this meaning man meets the meaning of the Word of God. The word of man, representing his experience and its meaning, needs the Word of God in order to be judged, purified, and complemented. And the Word of God needs the word of man in order for it to be understood as the Word of God.

In this dialogical ministry of preaching, the layman's role is most important and strategic. The clergy's role is an assisting one and is dependent upon the laity. The minister's sermon, as we have seen, is never heard outside the church walls as it is preached. It escapes into the world through the ministry of the laity who communicate it by word and action. They are the true ministers of the church because they live in the world where the church's mission is. Of course, it is true that an ordained minister should live in the world, too. His major responsibility is with the gathered church, however, unless he has a special vocation that indicates otherwise. It is his responsibility to train and direct, through the assistance of his people, the ministry of the church in its dispersion.

The gathering of the church as something special and separate is only momentary. Its permanent residence is in the world where the people really live. The church does not send people into the world; they are already in the world. It would be better to say: They go back from whence they came, namely, the world. We "come" to church in order that we may "go" as the church. We hope that in our gathering together as a special group in the name of our Lord we may be strengthened for our true life and service which in his name we render where we live and work and play.

All the people of God are agents of the ministry of the church. The ordained members are called not to do the work of the church for the people, but to train and direct the people's implementation of it. When, therefore, we say that the duty of the ordained minister is to preach the Word and administer the Sacraments, we mean to preach the Word in such a way that it activates its meaning in the lives of the people so that they engage the meaning of the world with the meaning of the Word. And the administration of the Sacraments does not mean to fulfill the priestly function of the church for the people of God, but to lead them in this ministry in such a way that the power of God becomes available to all men through their lives. All the people of God—ministers and laymen—are called to be the initiators and administrators of the dialogue between God and man in order that the Word-world encounter may continue the reconciling work begun by God in Christ.

APPENDIX

The précis that follows is of a sermon preached in a local church, and the transcribed discussion is that of a group of church members (three adults and three high school students) who gathered to discuss the service and the sermon immediately afterward. Both the sermon and the discussion are typical of many that the Institute of Advanced Pastoral Studies has recorded.

Précis of the Sermon

Text: The story of Jacob wrestling with the man. Gen. 32:24 ff.

In this scripture story, Jacob is a man who cannot sleep because he remembers his past: his scheming with his mother against his brother Esau; his plotting to get the birthright that was his brother's; his dishonesty and lying; the anger of his brother Esau; his flight from home. Now, twenty years later, he is confronted by all his past as he journeys back to meet his brother. And Jacob is afraid. Then, there comes a stranger, a man who wrestles with him until the breaking of day. Jacob refuses to let this stranger go until he blesses him.

It has been the experience of endless generations that man feels a restlessness in the presence of evil and is forced to battle through the night to discover what is right.

All of us wrestle in the darkness against a variety of selves: (*1*) the old self which shames us and still seeks to control us; (*2*) the sensitive self that is quick to feel slight and rejection; (*3*) the compromising self that says, "I am going to get along with things as they are"; (*4*) the anxious self that dreads insecurity—loss of health, job, family.

But in Jacob's case, when God had a part, and the struggle was fought with divine help, then Jacob changed —he became Israel, the victor. And although Israel bore the mark of that struggle, the limp with which he thereafter went through life, he was a man who had respect not only from others but for himself.

No man can win a victory over the selves which pull him this way and that unless the heavenly Father takes part in the struggle. And when Jesus enters our lives, he gives us: (*1*) a new self for the old; (*2*) a new stature for the sensitive self; (*3*) backbone for the compromising self; and (*4*) presence for the anxious self.

"Even now, Christ is here; and in his presence there is power—power for all your needs."

Sermon Discussion

In the discussion group were Chuck, the leader, who works for a machine-parts producer and is the father of two children; Joyce, housewife, who has three children; Elmer, a salesman, who has two married children; and Beth, Dorothy, and John, high school students.

Afterward, the ministers from the Institute who also attended the service and heard the sermon listened to the tapes of this discussion by laymen.

What Did the Preacher Say to You?

Joyce: I feel he was saying that part of my restlessness is not just unique for me, but that all mankind faces this.

Beth: When he talked about "yourself" I connected it with pride. Maybe that is the reason I feel I can't talk to God. This is something that is going to have to be settled between God and me.

Dorothy: I have a struggle about people's hypocrisies. I get upset when I discover how people can say they're Christians but when they live their life, they're not really acting it. They may be good to other people, but in a lot of things that they control, they don't really lead good lives. For example, I'm studying education now and in Birmingham the statistics say that we give $754 per student and only 20 miles away in Detroit, there is $300 per student. And, there really is a difference in the quality of education. I don't think you're giving equal opportunity to all the people and it's our people and our church that are preventing this. They're saying they're Christians but they are not really giving all of themselves.

Elmer: I think what the preacher said to me was that each of us needs to be reminded periodically that there is an answer to the constant struggle which each of us has. As I listened I was reminded of the things I have been ashamed of—not serious things, but things I would like to live over. And the thought occurred to me, "Gosh, I struggled with myself on these occasions and had I heard such a sermon as we heard today and thought of the everlasting arms, which is really what he was saying, it might have made it easier for me then." I have no doubt that I will have similar experiences in the future when thought-lessly I will do something or say something for which I have regrets. So, this is a reminder and I expect to be reminded of these things again from time to time through contact with the church.

John: Gosh, I'm not really sure. I think I got more out of the prayer, the pastoral prayer, than anything else.

Dorothy: Me, too.

John: He examined different kinds of problems people have, like we're afraid, we have fear, anxiety and things like that. I think the sermon went into that a little deeper and I can't really explain it. I get the impression there's always a solution to our problems.

Joyce: I think the preacher was saying Christians are not meant to be self-satisfied; there is a struggle, it is always going to be a struggle. Whenever you face people, you have a responsibility as a Christian, but it was never meant to be easy.

Chuck: This is really what the sermon said to me: We really have no business being self-satisfied; we have no business judging people who say they are Christians and don't act that way; we have our own continuing struggle, and since we have our own struggles we are in no position to judge others.

Dorothy: It's not so much the judgment—it's our lack of progress. It almost seems like we're being useless.

Chuck: I believe it would be well to point out here that all three of these youths are senior high youngsters, and I think they have something to say.

Dorothy: I think youth is trying to find a big answer to the whole problem.

Chuck: Right now!

Dorothy: Yes, you want an answer. You know there's something wrong and you want something done about it, but the adults have lived through it and they know there isn't anything to do about it, so . . .

From the Background: Change is slow.

Chuck: On the other hand, Dorothy, this is one of the things that perhaps is wrong. The preacher said this morning that adults are too satisfied with the "old self" and the "old ways" and we just said, "Well, there isn't anything you can do about it." And, here we sit!

Joyce: The Christian compromise. You do this many times a day.

Chuck: The portion of the sermon concerning Christian compromise, Dorothy; is that what you're pointing your remarks to?

Dorothy: I don't really know.

Chuck: I'm wondering if you are saying, "I wish he had talked on a different subject; namely, the union of the church." [prayed for in the pastoral prayer]

Dorothy: I liked that part of the prayer. It meant something to me. As far as the sermon, I don't think he hit on the real problem. Maybe if he had talked more about that it would have come closer to the problem.

Joyce: But he has to talk on the personal problem. This union with the church will be with people and until we can settle some of the struggles we have, there is not going to be a really true union.

Chuck: Dorothy, when you speak of union of the church, what are you referring to?

Dorothy: So that all people are in fellowship with God and we don't have individual . . .

Chuck: The sects? Is that what you're talking about?

Dorothy: Yes. We're so different now; if we're all for the fellowship and love of God, why do we have to be so different?

Joyce: These differences are changing, though. Would

you want them to be completely erased? You do have the fellowship with God. All people have this but some people are more comfortable worshiping in a service where there is more ritual and some are not. Do you think this should all be abolished?

Dorothy: No.

Chuck: Don't you feel, Dorothy, that really if in spirit we could find ourselves unified, whether we call ourselves Methodist, Presbyterian, or whatever, it's not all that important? And I think now again the preacher speaks of this when he says, "Certainly let us not let the difference in a worship service or doctrine be all that important in our lives. Let us clear these things away from between us and God and then unity comes, whatever you call yourself."

Elmer: I think the subject of today's sermon is one that might have been given in any Christian church you can think of, because I don't know of any church denomination which wouldn't recognize precisely what the preacher said—the internal struggle. The one thing all Christian churches have in common is God and Christ and the everlasting arms, which is what he was talking about. The form of the service is the main difference between churches. I attribute less importance to the form than to the content of the service. The content among all the churches I have attended is essentially the same.

What Difference Do You Think the Message Will Make in Your Life, and Where Did It Touch You and How?

Elmer: I think some of us partially answered question two as we discussed question one. I stated how it touched me—it was a reminder of what I have been told many times. I don't think it will make any difference in my life at my age. This isn't new, but it's a refreshing reminder of a source of help which is always present if I think of it.

Beth: I think the kind of discussion we are having helps us.

Chuck: Perhaps this is something we should do more often—tie together morning worship service with evening MYF or church school or something.

Dorothy: The questions and the discussions help us find answers. If I had gone home right after the service, I would have gone home with the same ideas and same questions.

Chuck: I think Dorothy has a very good point. And the church in my lifetime, and I'm almost sixty, does not provide this interchange of ideas between the young and the adults. I think this is real important. I've never heard anyone say it just like Dorothy has.

Dorothy: I think it's better for us, too, to discuss it with adults. We have basically the same questions, and when we (youth) discuss it we agree on questions, but we don't find any answers.

Chuck: You must remember that this is good for adults, too. Communicating is a two-way street. You just can't sit there and listen to us. There must be an interchange or it's meaningless.

Beth: If they did that, though, it would have to be in small groups like this, because if I was in a large group, I would clam up.

Dorothy: Especially our Sunday school class. There's so many people. If we did this, it would have to be on a much more voluntary basis if people were interested. Even if we really are sincere and believe something, it's hard to say it and know people are sitting there laughing **at you.**

Chuck: I believe this is true. John, do you believe that
—do you find it easier to talk in a small group?

John: Yes.

Joyce: Do you really think they are laughing or do you
just feel a little embarrassed, or . . .

Dorothy: Not necessarily. I wouldn't care if it was so
small, like you could have five more young people here,
except they would have to be really sincere.

Chuck: Well, they probably wouldn't be here if they
weren't.

Beth: Not necessarily, because a lot of times it is good
to have someone sitting beside you to say, "I don't even
believe in a God, etc." because at least then you have to
defend and know what you feel and know what you believe.

Dorothy: Yes, but they have to be able to listen and be
attentive. Some of these kids—if they just half listen then
that wouldn't be any good either.

Chuck: I don't know if this will do any good for the
Institute for Advanced Pastoral Studies, but it's good for
us.

Elmer: I think it will.

Chuck: I think if I were a young preacher, I would
give a lot of thought to what Dorothy has said; namely,
the opportunity to get an interpretation of others, including adults, to help them understand their messages.

Dorothy: When you're listening to something you're
listening to stuff that puzzles you—when you come into,
like here, and you come to the guilt part, I didn't really
hear, I was so busy questioning what he said to me that
I missed what you said. You miss something.

Chuck: The preacher is at a disadvantage because he
is talking to you and he needs a feedback. That's our job.

Beth: I went to a church a couple of Sundays ago where

they had an open sermon. The preacher would give a sermon but at any time, a layman could say, "Wait a minute, I don't understand this," or "Explain what you mean." I know I didn't say anything because I was a guest but it really helped me a lot to have those other laymen talk. I think to have an open sermon like this once in a while would help a great deal.

Did the Preacher's Methods, Style, Language, and Illustrations Help or Hinder the Message?

Dorothy: I think his style has definitely improved. I went there about five times in a row. He's always talking about his friends. I know he has many friends, but after you hear about "my dear friend from so and so" so many times—they don't illustrate the point. I think today he talked about what he wanted to say, but he wasn't illustrating so many people or so many situations.

Beth: I always turn him off when he starts off with "my dear friend from some place."

Joyce: It affects me the same way.

Beth: I cry sometimes. Some of the stories are really tear jerkers, but . . .

Chuck: I think those stories are fillers and I agree with the girls. The Easter service had some and I thought they were inappropriate.

John: I think if he is trying to make a point, though, he should go into it a little deeper to what he's trying to get at.

Joyce: . . . not so many personal references.

Beth: Right. I like him to quote poems or authors which I think means more to people than "my dear friend someplace." Many people may be familiar with quotes. Some ministers have used popular songs and have quoted them, and a lot of people say "that's a good idea" and then they hear it's a pop record and they get kinda flustered.

Chuck: That surprises me because the illustrations never affected me that way. How about that? Well, preachers, mark that down!

Dorothy: Some are very good and inspirational, but you know, when you get so many inspirational ones, I feel I'm uninspirational.

Chuck: Now I think his reference to Polonius' advice to Laertes was real good and pertinent. I'm sure we all recognized that quote.

Joyce: It gives you something to think back to.

Dorothy: I don't understand about Pontius Pilate crying forty years later, or something. Well, how would we know that?

Beth: I think he was stressing the guilt factor there.

Chuck: Did you see *The Robe* last Sunday? This is the kind of thing he could have used as an illustration: Richard Burton's struggle and release. This is exactly the guilt complex, except that it was more serious than any of us will ever experience. But it's the same kind of thing. He finally saw the light and was released from a burden which would have killed him.

Did the Sermon and Worship Work Together and Reinforce Each Other?

Dorothy: I think they did.

Chuck: The prayer was marvelous and certainly tied into the sermon. As a matter of fact, I was really impressed with the entire service. The music was beautiful.

Joyce: Yes, I thought so, too. I think it would be good if we had young ministers come visit us more often. [laughter follows]

Dorothy: I couldn't help wondering if maybe it was because of this.

Chuck: You don't think they're trying to put on a show, now do you? [again laughter]

Joyce: I'm not saying that at all, because I think by and large, our services are very effective. I have never failed to receive something from the music, or from the prayer, or from something. I have never felt that it's been an hour that I haven't received. This one question we're coming to: In what ways did you help? I think maybe I tried to help—I was really paying attention to every word.

Chuck: You knew you were going to discuss the sermon, though.

Joyce: I'm sure I was helping him.

Dorothy: By being attentive. You were really listening and helping.

Joyce: Right. And in the right frame of mind!

Dorothy: Right. Sometimes I'm not.

Joyce: Sometimes you go with your problems and you don't leave them, and you're not receptive to what he's saying, and you leave thinking, "I didn't get anything" but this is not the preacher's fault. This is my fault, I feel.

Chuck: I think that's the answer. We were attentive. Lots of times I have left the service and said to myself, "I wonder what he said." Maybe he didn't say anything to me, but chances are my mind was on something the day before, or what I'm going to do Monday—that meeting at 9:30 is going to be a tough one. Or, have you got your homework done for tonight?

Dorothy: Right. I don't think I have ever gone to a sermon where I haven't concentrated through the whole thing, but I don't concentrate through the prayers, I know, a lot of times.

Chuck: I think that the prayers are the most meaningful. It makes a difference who is praying. Some do a real fine job. I'd like to ask the young people how they feel about this responsive reading. I know how I feel about it —it annoys me! It just seems like you drag it in by the heels and say, "Now we have responsive reading."

Dorothy: You have to stand up through this whole thing.

Joyce: Maybe if we were more aware of what it was supposed to mean to us and why we do it, it might be more helpful.

Chuck & Dorothy: It's the Scripture.

Joyce: Didn't the early Christians go to church singing, and didn't the priests chant something and they would sing back, and this is where our responsive reading comes from?

Chuck: The Lutherans do this. They sing.

Joyce: But I think in our church we have the carry over in our responsive readings.

Chuck: In our service, aside from the text of the sermon, we get no Scripture except through the responsive reading. I think responsive reading is probably the least meaningful part of the service. My point is, does it contribute really to what you get out of the service? It doesn't for me and it never has. I have often wondered if this is something that's carried over traditionally—and since we're talking to young preachers, maybe they should give this some thought and find out whether their membership really wants it. Does it do anything for the members? I'd rather hear the choir sing a second song.

Dorothy: My problem is that even though I have a very large vocabulary, I find it a challenge to pronounce the words and I can't understand what a lot of them mean —not necessarily the Psalms, but in our old hymnal . . .

Beth: They're better in the new hymnal, but still many

of them don't mean anything to me. I kind of repeat what I'm supposed to.

Elmer: We follow these readings week after week, but there is no real tie-in between them and the Scripture and the sermon. At least, I've found it to be so. Beth's problem and my problem is that you're saying words and you don't have time to assimilate what the words are trying to say. I've stopped sometimes and thought, "What does this say?" and he's on the next verse and then it's my turn and I never get back to answer my own question.

Chuck: Are you suggesting that instead of the responsive reading, the Scripture that is to be used in the service would be more meaningful?

Dorothy: Yeah. Then you've got it in context and it means something.

Joyce: How about following along with your Bible?

Dorothy: Right. I think that would be good.

Beth: I think it would be helpful if they gave us time to get to the thing before they start reading.

Dorothy: One thing more about this. We've had guest preachers during Lenten services who asked if we would like to follow along in the Bible, and then they say "the verse is such and such." Quite a few of them do, and, I'm there without a Bible!

Chuck: Why would you? Today, for example, he read the text: "Jacob was left alone, etc." so you could follow that from the Bible, but you don't have to because you've got it right here.

Joyce: This would be in place of the responsive reading.

Dorothy: So you would correlate more into the sermon.

Elmer: I wish the minister had read the whole story of Jacob wrestling with the angel so I could have had a background for understanding the sermon.

Chuck: That's a good point.

Elmer: You had to know the story to know why Jacob was wrestling with himself. You probably knew the story, but I imagine there were a lot of people who didn't.

Beth: I didn't know the story.

Dorothy: I didn't, either.

Joyce: See, this is where the background would have helped out.

What Advice Do Any of You Have for Preachers and Their Communication?

Dorothy: One thing: find a style between the very informal and very formal, something that's a lot closer to what the people are used to. Have it free. Say a lot in it—have it informal, but not too informal, because it's religious.

Chuck: Do you feel the preacher today was too formal? I couldn't improve on his delivery or choice of words. I think he is an outstanding preacher. Some sermons are much better than others, but his batting average is better than any man I've ever heard.

Joyce: His sincerity comes through.

Elmer: One thing: Preachers make too many points. They come up to a point and really drive it home. I'm ready to bow my head and pray because I think we're all through. Then, boy, they start off on another attack. I've had that happen to me so many times. Then you've lost the whole *smear*.

Joyce: I agree. I've seen it happen many, many times. They make their point, but they seem to have to go right on.

Elmer: Yes, they oversell. As a peddler, I find this is disaster. I'd like to ask the young people a question. What was your reaction when the minister waxed emotional and his voice quivered? I don't like it.

Chuck: I don't think he can control this. I think it really gets to him.

Dorothy: He puts himself so "into it." Like that Easter thing. I sat through it twice and there wasn't a change in the pitch or anything.

Joyce: I have a different feeling. I think it's an advantage to be an actor, but I guess sometimes I wonder about it in a preacher.

Chuck: I think he's just so involved.

Joyce: I think this is true sometimes, but because of my makeup, I can't feel it's this way all the time.

Chuck: Then you would say to these preachers, "If you wax emotional—watch it!" I have a question I would like to ask all of you. In our church we range all the way from what you would perhaps call the real down-to-earth fundamentalists to the other end of the scale with some rather liberal people in the congregation. From time to time, the preacher issues altar calls. What is your reaction to this?

Elmer: I've never seen anyone go up, and I don't think you will in our congregation.

Beth: I don't think it has to be a public thing. My personal feeling is that if I give my life to God, it's between God and me. If it doesn't show in my relationships with people I'm with, then going to the altar isn't going to help it any because I'm not living through it anyway. I always feel that going to the altar is saying, "Hey, look at me, boy!"

Elmer: I agree with Beth one hundred percent, and I'm glad to hear a young person say this. I've felt this way all my life.

Dorothy: Chuck, when we had that woman evangelist, didn't you go up?

Chuck: I went up only because my boy was up there. She called for young people and asked the parents to follow. My youngster was up there so I went. I'm kinda with Elmer. This kind of approach doesn't really appeal to me. On the other hand, I sense that it does have meaning for some people.

Beth: I hate to say it but I think for some people it's a crutch; this is what they need, so I think they should have it.

Chuck: I wonder if this discussion about altar calls is helpful to the ministers from the Institute.

Elmer: I think it is. It very well could be since it is an example of one kind of thing we do in church that is out of date.

Chuck: The whole thing we have agreed on here pretty much is that the sermon, of course, is just one part of the over-all worship service, and we're striving to seek here what really is most meaningful and can be most helpful. I think this idea of dialogue after the sermon would be great if we could work something out and I don't see any reason why we can't.

Author's Comment

The foregoing sermon, typical of the kind preached in many local churches, is primarily concerned with the problems of individuals to the exclusion of any consideration of their environmental involvements and responsibilities. Because it deals with individual problems abstractly and without adequate reference to specific situations, it leaves the listener undirected and disoriented. Such sermons are theologically naïve and simplistic, and they produce theologically untrained and unsophisticated laymen. Yet this sermon is a sample of what many congregations hear from week to week.

In this discussion of the sermon, the church members, both the teenagers and the adults, attempt to react to the sermon and the service of worship. Some observations on their discussion are readily made:

First, the members of the group appreciated the opportunity to react to the sermon. But observe that the sermon influenced them more because they were able to discuss it.

Second, the range of interest and subject matter covered was greater in the discussion than in the sermon. The discussants' participation, therefore, broadened and deepened the scope of the message received as compared with the message delivered.

Third, the quality of the discussion—the level of knowledge and understanding revealed by the group—is not very great. Yet as such discussions go, it is average. Here is revealed the illiteracy and lack of religious depth that are to be found among a vast number of church members owing partly to the quality of the preaching and teaching in local churches and partly to lack of opportunity afforded laymen to deal responsibly with the teaching and preaching they do hear.

Fourth, both sermon and discussion reveal that there is need for more dialogue between pulpit and pew.